BE DELICIOUS

The ONLY Book You Need to Get a GREAT Voice

By Tracy Goodwin

Copyright 2010
All Rights Reserved

ABOUT THE AUTHOR

I'd like to tell you a little bit about myself and why I wrote this book before we get to work. I have a lot of education, more than I know what to do with. With that education I have learned so much that I really feel led to share what I've learned with others so they can benefit from it. I have upper level degrees in Directing, Creative Drama and Corporate Communications. However, I believe it is actually my years of practical experience working with all different types of students that has really taught me the most. It is work I've done with students just like you, combined with my education that has created the framework for this technique that will improve your voice, your movements and make you an outstanding communicator of casual conversation, public speaking and acting.

As a high school student I participated in speech, debate and drama. I went to many high school speech tournaments and won many awards. I was destined to be a star! After working as a professional actor for over 10 years and I'm proud to say making my living acting, I longed for more. I went back to school and got a master's in Child Drama and directed children's theatre all over the world for several years, but still, I knew I had not found my niche yet.

At that time I went to work for an acting conservatory teaching voice and movement; that is where the journey truly begins. I continued to see semester after semester, session after session, students making the same mistakes. I saw how the simplest techniques were keeping students from succeeding whether it was getting the part, or sinking the deal. It was at that time that I really began to hone in what it was that students needed to do in order to succeed by maximizing their voice and body. Alas, the delicious communication program was born. There could be no more "on" but only real life deliciousness. Now, after years of one on one consulting with pageant contenders, actors, lawyers, doctors, public relations people, and business associates all over the world I see just how anyone and everyone can easily become delicious.

This book is not directed specifically at actors or business people or radio personalitics. I mention all of the above but each person, whatever career, whatever purpose you are looking for help with, this book will help you. It is necessary for you to apply the exercise according to your audition, your business presentation, your one-on-one communication and so forth. But it is the same technique for anyone, regardless of what you do, your final goal will be the same. The actor will become a better actor and will do better in auditions. The business person will find him or herself nailing more presentations. The beauty pageant contender will find the interview portion much easier and their own performance much more successful.

SPECIAL THANKS

Thank you for buying this book. Trust me; you will thank yourself in a very, very short time.

Every voice instructor that I had the pleasure of studying under or working with, you gave me the foundation to create this theory of voice improvement.

Dorice Goodwin
Jack Paschall
Adam Tyler

and Toni Phelps, editor

TABLE OF CONTENTS

Introduction

A Note About How to Practice

Why Do I Sound Like This?

Voice

How To Breathe
(Rib Expansion Breathing)

The Big Three
(Pitch)

The Big Three
(Volume)

The Big Three
(Speed)

How to Give Emphasis
(Operative Words)

Inflection

Pausing

Elongation

How to Be Understood (Articulation)

Slang/Slur

Idiosyncratic Sounds and Words

Dialects

Movement

Posture

Gestures

Face

Eyes

Casual Conversation

There Is Always More Work...

INTRODUCTION

Welcome to Be Delicious Voice and Movement. This book will train you to maximize the true great qualities of your voice and body and integrate the two so that you will find more success as an actor, business person, speaker etc...

Everything in this book must be mastered if you want to finally and forever have a fantastic voice, wonderful movements which include posture, gestures, facial expressions and eyes that can reveal your heart and get you what you want.

It is also important that you master one element at a time in order to create a strong foundation that will be unshakable no matter what is thrown at you, this is the ultimate difference between really having a great voice and having an "on" voice, we will get to that later. The elements I teach you in this book are similar to children's building blocks and each element will be stacked one block at a time. When you have learned and mastered all of the elements you will have a wonderful, unshakable tower of communication skills that will not only help you nail the audition or the presentation but help you win in life. This technique works, this technique cannot be accomplished overnight so you must start right away and you must start at the beginning and you must also learn every single element not just the ones you like or think you need. Trust me, it is most probably that you need to learn all of the elements in the book or they would not be here.

This book is titled Be Delicious; it is

a book about getting a delicious voice. Now, what is delicious you ask? Have you ever met someone who had an incredible voice; something about them made you want to listen to them forever? A person who when they walk in the room all of their movements flow like water? A person who you, the first time you have a conversation with them, makes you feel as if you have known them forever? A person who when they make a presentation or give a speech you can't take your eyes off of them or stop listening and your mind never wanders? That is delicious; trust me, that is what you want. It is delicious that nails the audition or is a great actor or gives winning presentations or gets the girl and so on.

There is a lot of work to do, but the techniques I will teach you are super simple and easy to follow and you will see results pretty quickly. However, I'm not there to make you do it, you have to take the initiative and do the work. Trust me, after all these years of teaching this technique to hundreds of people, I can honestly tell you the only people who have not achieved tremendous success are the ones who did not finish reading, did not practice, did not do the exercises, and did not work the program. Those who did all of those things found great success.

A Note About HOW TO PRACTICE

Often times I get criticized on my videos when people do not completely understand what I am trying accomplish through over exaggeration in the practice exercises. But, when you are practicing, I want you to over emphasize unless otherwise stated. Now, in real life I don't want you to do that. In the pageant interview I do not want you to over emphasize, please understand this is a practicing technique. In real life, most of us do not over emphasize, so in real life I DO NOT want you to. However, as I train your voice to do something totally different, it is essential that you over emphasize all of the elements so that they will set, kind of like wet concrete.

Imagine a horizontal line with three vertical lines, one on each end and one in the middle. The line furthest to the left represents an average voice or perhaps where your voice is right now. The line furthest to the right represents maximum or over emphasized voice. The line in the middle represents exactly where we want your voice to be. When your voice settles into the middle line, you have achieved your goal. But, in order to get the vocal elements I am teaching you to settle, you have to over emphasize when you practice. It is necessary for you to push your voice all the way to the far right so it will stretch, like a muscle. Your voice has to learn something entirely new. Your voice has been the way it is now for a very long time, maybe 10, 20, 30 years or more. It will not change overnight or with minimal pushing. As you continue to push to the far right line, exaggerate, your voice will begin to free up, understand where it is going, and start to get the hang of the stretch. Once your voice has the hang of it and has been trained, it will start to settle in. On its own, it will settle back to the middle line and become a part of who you are, your new delicious voice. This is where it becomes essential for you to trust me. I am not teaching you to sound like an over emphasizing idiot, I am training your voice, and this is the way we are going to make the changes necessary for you to have a delicious voice.

When you are ready to practice your new skills on someone, make sure that you pick safe people. By this I mean people who will be supportive of what you are doing and not be critical or tell you things that are opposite of what I am telling you. Do not practice with people who are going to give you a hard time, be negative, criticize or try to tell you to do it different than what this text is telling you.

I tell you this because of experience. In the past, especially when I work with accent reduction students I have seen them give up because of comments from people they practice with. An example of this would be as follows; say I am working with someone on accent education that was born and raised and lives in the Bronx. Now, in case you do not know, and I am not being critical I am being honest, people from the Bronx have a reasonably thick accent. When they start learning and speaking with a standard American dialect they begin to sound totally different. Now, if this student from the Bronx happens to practice around their Bronx friends and family members, guess what happens? The new sound is very foreign to the outsiders and it sounds completely wrong and ridiculous to them. The outsiders or persons who also speak in a Bronx dialect refuse to accept what they hear coming out of my students mouth and whether they mean to or not, they tend to criticize and make fun of the work my student is doing. Guess what happens next? You got it. The student no longer wants to work on reducing their accent, which often times is something that they had wanted to do for years. If anyone criticizes what you are doing, IGNORE them, and as the old saying goes, maybe they will go away!

Strength, power, confidence, intelligence; that is what you want to exude, and yes, part of it is a state of mind. You have to believe that you are all of those things, but the elements listed above are mere techniques that can create these things. Even if you do not believe them now, you will after you've completed the exercises in this book and have created your new delicious voice. So as you are working on mastering the voice techniques, but these elements and techniques might also feel very strange to you and things may not sound right to you. I will tell you a phrase now that I want you to remember as you are learning...actually, forever..."fake it until you make it." What I mean by that is, no matter what you believe about your voice you must fake that you believe differently. It is imperative that you fake that you have a fabulous voice because if you do this, "fake it until you make it," while you are implementing these vocal tools and mastering the technique something amazing will happen. Now, please do not misinterpret what I'm saying, by saying "fake it until you make it" I'm NOT saying I want you to be fake, in fact that is one of the biggest problems with pageant girls' voices especially. Movements, facial expressions and gestures also tend to be fake. What I need you to fake is being natural and incorporating natural elements into your voice so then they *become* natural and automatic. Make sense? I will talk more about the difference between faking it and being fake or "on" a little later in the book.

It is also possible that you will be working very hard and thinking to yourself, "Gosh, I do not know if I am getting this. I do not want to have to keep thinking about this stuff, it is a lot to remember." Keep thinking about it and working on it and then I promise you, out of nowhere, one day, sooner than you think, all of the elements will just naturally be a part of you, you will not have to think about them anymore.

BEING "ON"

Before I break things down step by step I want to tell you something about speaking that you very well might do and have to change. Remember the goal of all auditioning, acting, public speaking and casual conversation is to appear natural, to be interesting, to make people want to listen because we have something to say, to make people believe we are interested in communicating with them and more. In way too many communication situations whether casual, interviewing, auditioning, presenting and others, we mentally tell ourselves, okay, I've got to be "on"...well, that's fine but what happens when we get "on" is this- we throw out all of the elements of naturalness in our voice and our body by trying to be interesting.

What it is that we are trying so hard to achieve does not stand a chance of happening, you may think it is, but when you get right down to it, it is only the illusion of being a great communicator. I want you to *really* be a great communicator, actor, auditioner, and so on, not just the illusion of one. So even if you think, well, when I'm "on" I'm a great speaker, great actor, great at auditions; you have to get that out of your head. "On" is NOT natural and not real, but rather rehearsed and forced. But most importantly, being "on" and the things you think you can accomplish when you are, are not as reliable as you think. So instead of working on your "on" we have to get rid of your "on" and make you real with a great real voice and great body language.

Example: Why doesn't the actor get the part so many times after the audition? Well, it's possible that he does not fit the role or is not that talented but many, many times it is because the actor "auditions" and all the elements that he/she creates with his/her voice in real life disappear. What is it that actors are supposed to do? Recreate real life. Therefore, it does not work when they become "on" because they actually become affected, like they are forcing all the good voice and movement qualities, like they are hitting me over the head with "hey, I am really doing a bang up job communicating this right, don't you get it?" Being "on" is fake and tense and it is not interesting or mysterious or by any means delicious. The same thing happens to people making presentations, lawyers, doctors, everyone really. For you it is often times when you are making casual conversation and even more often when you are in the interview process. You get "on" and as a result could not be less natural. Really delicious conversationalist and speakers are very natural; they do not get "on." Being "on" is absolutely the worst thing you can do. It is essential that you get rid of that concept right now. There is no such thing as "on." Being "on" is not successful, not reliable, and it is not real, therefore "on" mode cannot express all of the things you need to express both during casual conversation and during the interview process.

The people that we often times refer to as good speakers do not do any of that. They have the technique to do it differently. Now you are going to get the techniques that good speakers use, and trust me, it is not staring at the audience and imagining that they are in their underwear! It is the elements that I am about to teach you.

Exercise One

Make a list of anyone and everyone you think is a good speaker. If you are an actor, make a list of the actors that you think do really great work. You can comprise your list of anyone, it does not even have to be official speakers like the President of the United States or actors like Daniel Day Lewis. Your list can be comprised of anyone who is memorizing because of what they do with their body, their voice, their speaking and presentation ability. Of course Gandhi and Martin Luther King are good speakers, they can be on your list, but your friend Samantha or your

high school literature teacher can be on the list as well. Once you have your list formulated, next to each person's name write a few key words as to why you think they are a good speaker or actor.

Example: Speaker name--honest, friendly, courageous, integrity and so forth.

Writing Space for Exercise One

Okay, after you have completed Exercise One take a look and see if the people you wrote on your list execute any of the skills that you want to exhibit?
How many of those skills do you already utilize on a daily basis?

Let's get to work on your voice.

VOICE

There are only six things you have to master to create an interesting, exciting, commanding, and oh so delicious voice. These six things are:

- Utilizing proper breath support.
- Understanding and emphasizing operative words.
- Knowing how to play with your pitch both high and low.
- Understanding and utilizing the power of speed both fast and slow.
- Creating mystery with volume both loud and soft.
- Getting the words out of your mouth with clear articulation.
- Getting rid of slurring and slang.
- Getting rid of idiosyncratic sounds.

- Reducing dialects.

In my opinion, a voice should be like an orchestra; beautiful to listen to, interesting, unpredictable, commanding and loving and everything that music is to so many. By learning how to do the above six things, you will be able to create a vocal orchestra.

Now, with that said, let's talk about your real life voice, here and now. Think in terms of everyday life, the voice that you use when you speak to your family and closest friends, no pressure, no judgment, no pressure; for the most part unconditional love kind of folks. That is the voice that we want to start with and work on. That is the voice that must be the core in all of our communication affairs. First start out by thinking about how you are, how you speak when you are with your friends. I choose friends because sometimes you are more you with your friends then you are with your family, but you may certainly replace friends with family, anyone that you are completely and totally comfortable being yourself around.

Exercise Two

Spend a few hours/days/weeks paying attention to your vocal patterns. What I mean by that is, how do you speak, how do you sound, what does your voice naturally do when you are with your friends, spouse, relatives, anyone that you feel comfortable with? This can be in person observations or on the phone. Write down your thoughts

Writing Space for Exercise Two

What I want you to notice is how your voice has a certain rhythm, sound, and color to it that is all very natural. You naturally speak with high sounds, low sounds, and you speak fast and slow, loud and soft. You emphasis certain words over others, and you do it naturally, and automatically and it is great. That is what you have to learn to do all the time and it is *that* voice that we are going to enhance and make better.

This theory of using the voice you have right now, the voice you don't like, will work even for the person who is very quiet and shy and monotone. We will be enhancing this voice; this is our foundation. The person who is monotone or loud or has any type of voice will succeed with these elements because you are going to be bumping everything up, enhancing everything you already do and learning new skills to add to the foundation you already have. If you have a specific problem, as we go through the elements, you will see how you simply have to incorporate the opposite.

Example:
If you are too loud, we have to work on your soft.
If you are monotone, pitch is going to be important for you.
If you are shy, breathing will be essential.

I will give you all the elements, but since I am not there with you, to do a voice analysis of you before you start, then it will be very important for you to honestly take a look at your voice, your weaknesses and yes, your strengths because I assure you that you do have them. It is just human nature to focus on the negative. If you can't figure out your vocal qualities on your own, then ask for help. It is from that analysis that you will begin to see which elements you are missing, which ones you need to pull back on, and the areas where you need to incorporate something.

Okay, so after you have paid attention to your speech pattern for a day or two with people you are comfortable with, it is time to spend a little time looking at what happens to your voice when you are around people or situations that you are not comfortable with.

Pay attention to what happens to your voice when your uncomfortable, I'm not talking about getting specific emotions but rather being in situations and people you don't like or don't feel comfortable with, situations in which you feel on the spot or feel too much pressure or have to be around a boss or co-worker that you just don't get along with. What happens to your voice in those situations?

Exercise Three

For a day or a week, pay attention to your voice. See what happens to your voice in uncomfortable situations and write down your thoughts.

Writing Space for Exercise Three

Okay, so now we know what we are working with.

Now the moment you have been waiting for, let me tell you what we want to work for and balance is KEY.

Now, I am not a psychologist but there is an element of psychology that goes into having a great voice. The voice that we speak in is our voice because of our physical make up and where we place our voice, but it is also our voice because of the life we have. What do I mean by this? We speak the way we speak because of the experiences we have had in our lives.

This is more food for thought than anything else and I am not going into great detail about it but many people do not speak in their real voice.

Everyone has a real voice, the voice that they were originally meant to speak with. Most people do not speak in their true voice or even know what it is. The voice that most people speak in is a voice that is compensating for something; some experience that occurred that changed how you choose to speak. This can be something that evolved over years and like I said before, most of the time, you, the speaker, are not even aware of it. Speaking in this voice that is not truly ours explains so many of the vocal qualities that we have or rather do not have. The un-real voice tends to be more strained, less interesting, more one dimensional, not that your real voice cannot be these things but the not real voice almost always is.

Example:

I worked with a student one time who I could barely hear. He was very soft spoken and I often times had to ask him to repeat himself. Well, guess why he wanted to work with me? He wanted to be louder, to be heard, and to have more power and presence. As I worked with him I learned that he was the youngest child of 7 AND the only boy. Well, that was all I needed to know. Poor guy, he never got a word in edge wise. But, with correct breathing and some vocal technique in a few short weeks he was being heard and I am not just talking volume!

If you suspect that you are not speaking in your true voice, vigilance with the pitch work will help you get back to using the voice you are meant to speak with.

I can also say to you that your adjusted voice is possibly related to self-confidence issues. So it would be great for me to say, just be confident. I can say just be confident, but I also know that statement is much easier said than done. What we really have to say is, do the work, improve your voice through technique, and that will improve your self-confidence. Then your true voice can, and will, re-surface again.

How to Breathe
Rib Expansion Breathing

Now, you're probably saying, "What? I just paid 21 bucks for a book and this woman is talking about breathing, I do that involuntarily!!!" What does that have to do with anything? Well, ummm…everything! If you do not breathe properly, your body cannot work properly. Once you stop breathing you muscles tense up, even if you don't add stress into the mix. Once your muscles tense up, your voice can't work properly which means you cannot create a delicious sound because the sound is coming out of a place that is tense and restricted. Now, if you were in my class right now I'd go into a pretty huge to do about breathing. In fact, I would spend days on it, but I'm not going to spend days on it, I'm just going to give you the basics. Because it is the first thing I'm talking about, it's OBVIOUSLY important. If it is not obvious, well, heads up, this is important!

Okay, so almost everyone on the world does not breathe...well, we do but we don't.

Exercise Four

For a day or two, pay attention and see how many times you can catch yourself holding your breath or breathing shallow. By breathing shallow I mean taking in small lung breaths. You will be shocked. It might be beneficial to see the actual number in writing.

Writing Space for Exercise Four

There are statistics and research that prove what I am about to tell you, it is not something that I just made up willy nilly.

Humans, especially Americans, are under so much stress that we automatically hold our breath without even realizing we are doing it. Just pay attention and you will see; you hold your breath on the train, in the car, at work, all the time. In the pageant competition, especially the interview section you are probably experiencing a high level of stress and pressure. What do you do when you're under stress? You hold your breath, no ifs ands or buts about it.

First and foremost you have to stop holding your breath. You have to breathe, even if you do it wrong! So start breathing. Make a conscious effort, at first, to just make sure you are breathing. Once you can remember to breathe, you can learn to breathe properly.

Now I want to talk about right and wrong breathing, and the fact that the majority of people breathe wrong. We don't take in enough air which is one of the main reasons our voices can't do interesting things. Without maximum amounts of air, the voice does not have the breath support it needs to be delicious, to be strong, to be loud, and to be interesting etc... Get in a huge argument with someone and see how many times you have to take in deep breaths. You take in the air in those moments because you want and need the power to yell, to scream, to cry, to make your point and get what you want, right? Just say yes.

Okay, now I want to discuss how you, I, and all of us breathe wrong. It's not our fault, society did it to us! Magazines, television shows, movie stars, celebrities, fashion all of them are to blame, but also our parents and grandparents. We can blame everything else on them, why not this!

This is what has happened. Society has always taught men that they have to puff up the shoulders and walk tall, look macho and tough. For women, society says suck in your stomach and look thin. In addition society says tall women that they should not be, so they slump over and short men should be taller, so the crank they shoulders and neck back. This scenario is especially true for the pageant contender, model and often times actors. "Think beautiful, like the magazine cover" is ingrained in your head. Well, guess what, all of this is wrong because if you are holding your body in any of these fashions listed, which I can tell you, 96 percent of you are; you can't breathe properly. NO WAY, NO HOW! But, I can teach you to breath and it won't affect or destroy the look you are trying to achieve, in fact it will only work with your body to achieve a more relaxed look which is what we are ultimately going for.

Now, do not get me wrong, you still breathe, of course you do or you would die, but what ends up happening to all of you is that you just use a portion of your lungs to take in air and breathe. Now I know your saying, "Ummm, Tracy, don't be so stupid, that is what the lungs are for, duh." Well, yes, but you cannot get maximum power by just breathing through your lungs. Stay with me for a minute because that is just one of the wrong ways to breathe.

Now let's look at the folks, lots of them that were in choir or are singers and learned to breathe through their diaphragm. Well, they are one step ahead of those of you that are lung breathers only, but in a perfect world of delicious voices, they are still NOT breathing completely right. (And the choir teachers around the world gasp in collective horror). Trained singers are breathing through there diaphragm which is the box below the lungs and does hold more air than the little bit of lungs that the rest of you are using to breathe and the diaphragm does have power than lung breathing, but guess what, there is still a better way! After all, in your swimsuit or evening gown you cannot have your belly pouching in and out, period, right? In addition, when you are nervous, if you are lung breathing, your chest is heaving up and down. I do NOT think that you want the judges to see that!

If you want to achieve maximum power, maximum breath support, the ultimate amount of air to become delicious extreme, then you have to learn to breathe through your rib cage! Say what? Yes, it is called rib expansion breathing. You have to learn to take in air and release it from the rib cage. It has the biggest capacity to hold air and will give you supreme breath support so your voice can do everything you want it to do.

Okay, great! So how do you do that? Well, before I tell you, I want you to visualize something. Do any of you remember Jello 1-2-3? I might be showing my age, but when I was growing up there was a Jello product called Jello 1-2-3. In my six year old opinion, it was the greatest thing ever invented. It was Jello, but it had three different colors, three different layers one on top of the other. Let's say it was a red version of Jello 1-2-3. In that case the bottom layer was dark red, the middle layer was medium red, and the top layer was light red. I suppose you might get the same idea visualizing other food items that are similar but try to visualize my Jello 1-2-3. I want you to think of the three different colors of Jello as representative of the lungs, the diaphragm and the rib cage. When you eat the Jello, you first eat the lightest layer, the layer on top which represents the rib cage. Then you move on to the middle layer and eat it, the middle layer represents the diaphragm. Lastly you eat the bottom layer, the dark red, which represents the lungs. So when you eat the Jello, you eat the top layer completely, then the middle layer and finally the bottom.

Rib expansion breathing is the same concept. You fill the rib cage with air first, then move on to let air fill in the diaphragm and lastly the remaining air fills in the lungs. This all should take place in each breath. Do you see now how you have three vessels full of air rather than one small one? So instead of taking in a little bit of air in your lungs and trying to make get it to create an incredible voice, now you have lots and lots of air power because you have filled up all three. The air power that comes from the ribs and spills over into the diaphragm and lungs is going to allow you to create the elements of loud/soft, high/low and fast/slow which are critical elements in achieving a delicious voice.

Okay, great… but once again you ask, HOW do I do it?

First lay down. No really, lay down. When you are lying down you cannot breathe wrong. When you are sleeping, your body does not have your mind telling your body to adjust because you are too tall or too fat or whatever it tells your body that adjusts your posture. Your body is allowed to breathe properly.

Exercise Five

Lay down on the floor or a bed and feel how it feels to breathe right.

Writing Space for Exercise Five

Now, while you are lying down, do not analyze what is going on, in fact, do not even think about it. What I want you to do is *feel* what is going on. By that, remember what it feels like. Feel what it feels like to breathe properly, trust me, you cannot feel this when you are standing up, not yet anyway!

Just a side note, everything we do, every event, **everything** is recorded into our muscle memory. We can recall every event that is stored in our muscles, forever. Where do you think the phrase "it is like riding a bike" comes from? That is what it means; that once you learned to ride a bike, you will never ever forget. Everything is that way. Breathing properly is no different, which is why I want you to feel what it feels like; because you will need to recall this feeling over and over again as you learn to breathe properly. Once you have done exercise four and you think you have a good understanding and sense of the feeling of proper breathing, I do not want the awareness to stop. Every single time you lay down at night pay attention to what it feels like and during the day start paying attention to how you are NOT breathing properly so that you can start to incorporate that feeling in the day as you learn to breathe correctly.

Now what we have to do is to recreate what breathing feels like when we are lying down while we are standing up.

This is a little more complicated to teach because I am not right there with you but I will explain it in very simple terms.

I want you to put your hands on your ribs and place a little pressure on them. This experience can work even better if you have another person to help you. If you do, have the other person place his/her hands on your rib cage and apply a little pressure. Take in a breath. When you take in your breath, the helper's hands, or yours, should be able to feel the ribs expand. Most likely the ribs will not expand too much at first. But hopefully you will feel some inkling of movement, in other words, expansion.

Now, do not panic, but I have to tell you there is a strong possibility that you will not be able to feel any expansion at first. I would say about 30 percent of the people I work with cannot feel anything the first time they try this technique. So, the best way for me to teach you how to make this happen and I would teach it to you this way if I were standing right there with you is this. You are going to have to go to visualization again. It is essential that you visualize taking in a breath from below, from down deep. Think of it as taking in a breath and the air is down at your toes and you have to pull it up. If you think of taking the air in through your mouth and into your lungs, which is exactly what you have been doing for years, then you will not be able to expand your ribs at all. Do not get discouraged, this is the hardest part of the entire set of skills you have to master. Think low, pull in from a deep place and when you can visualize that you will begin to do it. All that matters is that you can expand those ribs a teeny, tiny bit at first. Once you expand those ribs just a little bit, they know what it feels like and they can remember that feeling so that you can continue to recall it. Each time you recall the rib cage to expand, it will expand more and more. Rib expansion breathing is something I strongly recommend that you practice and work on every single day until you master it.

Exercise Six

Practice rib expansion breathing EVERY DAY!

Writing Space for Exercise Six

The manner in which I want you to practice rib expansion breathing is by taking in a breath to expand the rib cage and counting as you do it.

Example:

As you inhale, say one...two...three... and repeat the counting as you exhale, one...two...three.

You may only be able to take in a two count when you start, that's okay. Do it anyway, put those hands on your rib cage and breathe in and out while you are counting. Take in as much as you comfortably can, don't push it too far. If it is a two count, let it be a two count, then exhale, same thing, 1...2.

Tomorrow, try for 3 counts on inhale and exhale and the next day 4 counts and add one number every day, if you can. If you cannot, that is okay too. Let the goal be to reach the number 30. That sounds very far-fetched at this point, I know, but trust me, it is much more easily obtainable than you can imagine at this point.

Stay at a number count as long as you need to, do not rush ahead at the risk of not fully feeling the technique and getting it solid, like cement. It is also possible, just like when you are on a diet, that you will hit a plateau. Perhaps you quickly and easily get to a 15 count, then out of nowhere it becomes difficult to move ahead. That is okay, stay at 15 for a few days or weeks; however long you feel you need to. When you are ready to move on to a higher number you will know. Move along then, not before, in order to ensure success. As the days and weeks go by you will continue to add numbers counting up higher and higher, expanding those ribs further and further and then out of nowhere in thirty or forty five days, give or take, you will be inhaling and exhaling with a full understanding of rib expansion breathing, proper breathing to a count of 30 or more!!!!!

At this point you are on your way...yes...it can be done, hundreds of my students master rib expansion breathing easily and actually many of the students even make it past a 60 count. But you just worry about 30 for now. The only student who was never able to achieve and master this technique was the student who did not try at all. DON'T get discouraged! Take your time. I am asking you to change a lifetime of learned behavior, a lifetime of muscle memory, and that's not easy. Learning, fully comprehending, and executing rib expansion breathing cannot happen overnight. I repeat, it cannot happen overnight so do not try to make it so.

Rib expansion breathing is just like going to the gym and working out muscles. If you have never stretched your legs you can't just wake up one day and do the splits, it takes weeks and weeks of stretching those muscles out and then eventually you can do the splits. Learning this breathing technique is exactly the same concept. Your rib cage is not used to being expanded with this much air or possibly any air. It is going to take some time to stretch those muscles out which is why we start with a one count, not a thirty count. BE PATIENT.

When it is all said and done and you are breathing in and exhaling properly, you will be filling up the rib cage, followed by the diaphragm and the spillover of air will slightly raise the chest as it fills in the lungs. And boy, you will have some real air power to work with. Also, you will have so much air to work with that your muscles will easily relax on their own. This is a great technique to use in high stress situations. Let's face it, you are really in need of every bit of help you can get, every technique available to relax in this situation. I get excited just thinking about it!

Rib expansion breathing is important and essential for every person who wants to have a delicious voice, but as a pageant girl it is a MUST for you especially. If you want to be more interesting with your voice than the other 55 actors who are auditioning for the same role as you, then you need the air power to make your voice delicious.

Exercise Seven

Watch people on TV, actors, new casters, etc. Notice how their chest does not heave up and down in an extremely noticeable fashion when they breathe? At least that is the case with the good ones! Now watch yourself in the mirror and pay attention to your chest movement when you breathe. How much movement do you see in your chest? After your observations on yourself, observe your friends and family to see how they breathe. See any heaving?

Writing Space for Exercise Seven

So there you have it; correct breathing called rib expansion!!! Easy enough...now, let's move on for more deliciousness!

A note about Posture: I have possibly put the cart before the horse by talking about breathing before I talk about posture. The most important things about posture I have included in the beginning of the section on breathing, but for some of you, you want more, you want me to answer the question, what is good posture?

Once again, it can be linked to the puffing up of the shoulders and the sucking in of the stomach; those things are not going help achieve good posture. Back when I was younger we were taught to put a book on your head and walk, if you were standing up straight and had good posture you could keep the book on your head. But, even today, researchers have studied how that is still too erect, not what we truly call good posture. First, good posture is something that is truly comfortable, now it might not be when you first start incorporating it because it is something new and different. You have compensated with your posture just as you have with your voice. For whatever reason, the compensation has occurred over the years whether you know it or not. Instead of thinking of books on your head or shoulders back or anything like that I want you to visualize something to understand correct posture.

I want you to visualize a child's building blocks that he/she stacks up one on top of the other, like the blocks I talked about in the introduction. Children's blocks, if properly stacked, stay standing. The body is exactly the same; it stands properly if it is stacked one section on top of the other. The ankles should be stacked on top of the feet, the knees on top of the ankles, the hips on top of the knees, the back on top of the hips, the neck on top of the back and the head on top of the neck. If you stack correctly, you will be standing correctly, can breathe correctly and you will not topple over. If you do not stack properly you won't be able to stay stacked up and you will fall over. You will not truly fall over, but you will not be able to breathe properly or stand or sit or walk properly and this leads to issues down the line with mobility and more.

The best way to practice stacking

your body blocks is by standing with your feet spread a little apart, body relaxed and fall over, meaning bend over and try and touch your toes. Now, very slowly, you are going to roll up to standing. As you slowly roll up I want you to physically and mentally visualize your body stacking itself one section on top of the other.

If your back is arched or your hips are titled back or your neck or head is falling over then your blocks are not stacked properly. Make sure you see and feel the blocks stacked gently on top of each other. This is going to feel very strange at first but keep it relaxed, not tense, and you will get used to it.

Exercise Eight

Practice the roll up of building blocks to correct posture every single day.

When you feel like you are beginning to master correct posture when you are practicing, then start to be aware of it in real life and adjust every single time you realize you are not standing or sitting with proper posture.

Writing Space for Exercise Eight

THE BIG THREE

Pitch

Before I get into pitch I want to bring up two other vocal elements that can absolutely keep you from getting the voice you want. Hopefully I have made it clear that you have to have a beautiful voice all the time, not just sound like you know what you're talking about during the audition or the presentation but have a wonderful voice like an orchestra that everyone wants to hear. A voice that is enjoyable to listen to in speed and pitch and timber.

Two of the biggest problems with many girls voices, are nasality and little girl voice. I want to address both of those now because one of the best ways to improve both is in the area of pitch. Now, no doubt proper breathing can really help, especially in little girl voice but pitch and the mastery of pitch play or lowering pitch is essential.

When I speak of nasality I am talking about the voice that sounds like it is coming out of your nose, or perhaps you're pinching your nose closed when you speak. Okay, you're not really doing that but it sounds like you are.

The other is the little girl voice. Now, this is important because many girls think that the little girl voice is really cute and can get them what they want. Here's a really important tip; it can if you're five and it's your true voice. Otherwise, forget it. Your voice has to show that you are confident and in control and can handle anything that is thrown at you. The little girl voice does not express that. So, if you think it's cute and that it will get you what you want, you need to get that idea out of your head immediately, because it will do nothing but hurt you.

So, if you have nasality or little girl voice it is essential that you master the pitch section of the book. Pay very close attention to everything I say in this section.

I call the next set of things I will talk about, pitch, volume and speed, or the "big three" because they are possibly the three most important elements to master in creating a delicious voice.

Now, pitch. First, I want to talk about the person who does not use the "big three." That person is the college professor whose class you ALWAYS fell asleep in. The class that you hated going to because it was boring, did not make any sense, or was hard to follow. Well, a big part of that professor's problem is that he/she did not utilize the "big three," so when he/she spoke their voice was monotone. (Do all of their future students a favor and send them the link to buy my e-book).

The first of the "big three" that we will address is pitch. First of all, what is pitch? Pitch is the high and low sounds that your voice makes. The human pitch has a pretty broad range from very high to very low. Everyone talks in a certain pitch. Some people talk in a high pitch, some in a low pitch. That is the foundation of your voice. But what I'm talking about when I talk about pitch work is expanding the range of the pitch you use. Not just speaking everything in the same high pitch or low pitch but once again assigning value. Some things should get assigned high pitch, some low. By assigning highs and lows and speaking with a range, you become more interesting than if you keep everything in the same pitch and assign the same pitch value to all your spoken words, sentences, and thoughts.

Example:

Let's say you find out your friend is getting married, and you say "Oh My Gosh, that's so exciting!" Do you say that in your normal pitch? In the same pitch you would say, "Can I have a ham sandwich?" No you do not. Your pitch goes up a notch, or twenty, because you are excited. Emotion is one of the many things pitch represents. Pitch can help people understand how we feel. Pitch can make us unpredictable and interesting to listen to. So we need to utilize all of the pitch range we have in order to be the maximum of delicious.

Now, if you just read the above paragraph and your saying to yourself, "Well, I would not really use a higher pitch when I say that line, I would say it just like I say everything else," then this section is especially important for you. It is imperative that you broaden your pitch range.

Pitch is just like every element I talk about in this book. If you do not use it enough, we need to bump you up, if you use it too much, we need to pull you back. What I am ultimately trying to do with your voice is to create an interesting balance of all the elements. Because I am not with you, it is imperative that you are honest with yourself about what it is that you do, and what your true speech and vocal patterns are.

Exercise Nine

Pay attention to your pitch and how much high and low variation you use.

Writing Space for Exercise Nine

Now, if you ever took music lessons you probably remember vocalizing the scales up and down the piano. I am going to train your voice to do something very similar but not singing. I am going to teach you how to expand your pitch, which I will call range, so that you can use more of what you already have. Again, this is not singing so don't worry if your thinking, "wait a minute, I do not sing!"

First, let's have a visual. Think of a staircase. See the staircase and visualize yourself walking up and then walking down the stairs. When you go up or down the stairs, you physically pick up your foot/leg and step up or down. Now we are going to replace you, your foot/leg, with sounds. I want to start with vowels. In the voice that you generally speak in, every day speech, your natural pitch, I want you to say the letter "A." Now, hold the letter for a moment in your natural pitch. AAAAAAAAA. Now I want you take that A up the stairs so that each A that you say gets higher/sounds higher/is spoken in a higher pitch. When you do this don't hold the A out like your singing, like I had you do first but rather say the A then say it again after you have physically picked it up and placed it on the next step up. Think of physically moving the A up the stairs and with each step the sound of the A gets higher. Go as far as you can go up in pitch but don't push past that point. When you feel you cannot go any higher, you cannot take any more steps up with your A you will know it. Stop right there. At the point where you have stopped, say your A and hold it for about a count of three to five.

AAAAAAA Then, bring it down the stairs, meaning say A again as you pick up the A and physically move it back down the stairs, back to middle level or your natural pitch. Now repeat the same thing going down the stairs. Remember to pick the A up and physically take it down to the next level. Repeat the moving down the stairs scenario exactly the same as you did going up the stairs. Move the A as far down the stairs as you can then do not push any further. Stop, hold it out for a count of three to five and then physically pick it up and move the A back up to middle range, your natural pitch/natural speaking voice.

Exercise Ten

Repeat the above activity with each of the following vowels A E I O U up and down the stairs just as explained above

Writing Space for Exercise Ten

Once you start to get the hang of moving the letters up the stairs and down the stairs start to feel the pitch expanding and hear the different sounds that you are making. I want you to run the entire staircase in one set. Start at the middle pitch or your natural speaking voice. Pick up your A and move it up the stairs as far as you can go then pick it up and move it directly down the stairs as far as you can go, do not stop in the middle this time. Once you have made it to the bottom step then pick up your A and take it back to the middle, your natural pitch.

Once again just like the rib cage, expanding your pitch is going to be similar. You are expanding your pitch into areas that it possibly has not gone before, or certainly has not gone to on a regular basis. At first, you may not be able to expand your range very high or very low, that's okay. The more you do this activity the broader your range will be and that's what you ultimately want is a broad range in pitch. As you practice, push your staircase letter stepping it as far as you can but DO NOT overdo it. Expanding pitch is just like many of the elements in this book, it is not something you can completely change overnight, and it will take time. As you continue to practice this pitch expansion you will begin to feel and hear a broader range within your sound. Out of nowhere really your highs will become higher and your lows will become lower. These highs and lows give you a more delicious range than the highs and lows that you have always used and spoken with before.

Now, let me make just one quick note here. In order to do this activity, you have to breathe! So make sure you take in a good rib breath before you climb up the stairs or down the stairs or both. All of these voice elements that I am teaching you have to be combined with breathing; it is the foundation and without out your house will fall down!

Now let's briefly talk again about the person who is nasal. If you have nasality we need to get rid of it. The best way to do this is do extra practice on the down the stairs version of the pitch work. It is okay to go up the stairs vocally, but you need to do twice as many scales down the stairs. Think of it this way, you are pulling that sound out of your nose, you are pulling it downstairs.

If you have little girl voice, the downstairs exercises are more important as well and you should double up on down. You do not have to not do upstairs but you definitely have to do twice as much downstairs. Why? Because what is little girl voice? It is a high pitched voice. In order to get rid of it you have to strengthen the low pitch part of your voice. Half of the battle with this one will simply be getting used to hearing a different voice, probably your true voice. You have most likely mentally placed your voice up high because you mentally believe that the little girl voice will get you what you want, just like I said at the beginning of this section. But, your true voice is more than likely not even close to that high in range.

Look at it as a journey to discover

your true, rich and delicious voice.

Exercise Eleven

Ponder this...are you speaking in your true voice? If not, why not? What event changed that?

Writing Space for Exercise Eleven

THE BIG THREE

Volume

The next of the "big three" is volume and this is a big one. Many people talk too loud and many more people speak too softly, all the time. Many of my clients want to be heard and they think they are talking about volume, but they are talking about so much more. Many times soft speaking has to do with lack of confidence. Now I can't give you confidence, but I can teach you how to have a great voice from which more confidence will come. Basically what I have to do, especially for you soft-spoken ones, is teach you this technique. Remember, "fake it until you make it."

Now, some people naturally speak louder and some naturally speak softer as I said before. I do not think we have to take away what you have been doing, be it too loud or too soft. The problem arises if you do that all the time. Once again we must go back and look at balance and value. Everything does not warrant the volume of loud (New Yorkers take note) and everything does not warrant the volume of soft. Once again we have to begin to enhance our loud with soft and our soft with loud therefore creating variety.

Exercise Twelve

Pay attention to what you do most when you are speaking. Do you speak loudly too often or do you speak quietly too much of the

time?

Writing Space for Exercise Twelve

Volume variation is a big one as I stated before, but I think volume variation is the easiest of all the elements to master. Learning how to incorporate loud/quiet is simply a matter of being aware and making adjustments. Start to pay attention to what it is that you say; the words you speak that really deserve loud or really deserve a soft volume. But don't always be predictable. We automatically assume that when we are mad being loud is the way to get what we want. Well, guess what? It's not. I always get more attention when I'm mad and quiet.

Loud and quiet are the elements where we can really look at the voice and its link to expressing emotion. Emotions are delicious as well because there are so many shades of them. When we think of emotion we say, mad, sad and glad. However, each and every emotion has shades of that emotion. So when you want to express something, a feeling, you do it because you want something. You want a response. So first, you have to figure out which shade of the emotion you want to use and then assign the correct vocal volume to express that shade.

Exercise Thirteen

Make a list of every emotion you can think of, start with the ones that you use the most and then write down next to it the variations of it.

Example:
*anger: mad, seething, erupting, jealous, envy, rage and so forth

Okay, so you have your list of the emotions that you use and the shades of those emotions. I'm going to give you a list of sentences that I want you to practice by saying the sentences applying the different emotions vocally to the sentence. First round, do what you would normally do, meaning, say the sentences how you would say them if you were assigning mad or sad or glad or whatever emotion to them.

I can't believe you did that.

Now what are we going to do?

I just don't think I can work here anymore. It's not about the company, I've loved working here, but I just feel like it's time to move on.

If you don't get your stuff and get out of here now I'm going to go over the edge.

I love my dog so much, I just can't wait to get home and see her every day.

My mother is coming up for holiday and she is going to spend two weeks here.

I just won this crazy sweepstakes I participated in. They sent me a check for $40,000.00! Can you believe it?

She said that she doesn't want to see me anymore. She says it's not about me but that she has to go out and have some "me" time. What is that supposed to mean?

Okay, you have now said these sentences over and over applying different emotions to them and have said them out loud the way that you would normal say them.

Now I want you to say the sentences again and do just the opposite or assign a different vocal shade to the sentence, meaning you say it completely different than you said it the first time but still applying the same emotion.

Example: The first time you said the first sentence you assigned the emotion "anger" to the sentence and you vocally presented it by yelling. That was one shade of anger, maybe rage. Now I want you to assign a different shade of anger to that first sentence, maybe seething and say the line in a seething tone which is much quieter than yelling.

Try all of the sentences with different vocal variations based on different shades of emotions. You will quickly see just how much of your voice your not using, just how predictable you can be, and just how limiting it is not to use all the shades of emotions and shades of your voice..

Writing Space for Exercise Thirteen

Now hopefully you can clearly see how volume is about variety and variety is especially important for presentations, sales pitches or anytime you are trying to get what you want. Go in for the kill. How do you vocally go in for the kill? By giving them what they DO NOT expect. If you are like most people/presenters you are predictable. Don't be predictable. That is the most important thing I can tell you about loud and soft; use it, all of it, every shade of it, but DO NOT use it as people think you are going to.

What makes people interesting? The same thing that makes good movies interesting, they are unpredictable. You have no idea what they are going to do next. But you wait with anticipation to see don't you? Of course you do, we all do. Delicious voices create the same thing, anticipation; we want to listen to them because they are unpredictable and have so much interesting variety.

THE BIG THREE

Speed

Now let's move on to the final component of the "big three". Fast and slow. It makes sense to start this section off exactly as the section on loud and soft. Once again, you have a pattern, maybe you speak fast, and maybe you generally speak slowly. Same principle, whatever it is that you do, we need to bump up the opposite, create a balance, and assign value.

Exercise Fourteen

Pay attention to your speaking rhythm are you fast, slow, both? When are you each?

Writing Space for Exercise Fourteen

Now same principle as loud/soft, start applying fast and slow and once again, be unpredictable. In the situation when you would normally be fast, try being slow. Think back to the variety of, the shades of emotions, apply fast and slow to them. But, use both. Once again, guess what, it is about variety.

Example:

If you are really excited to tell your spouse about the promotion you got at work, then you are probably going to rattle off all of the information really fast. That is fine, but two things. One, it is predictable. Perhaps it might be more interesting if you mix in some slow and fast when revealing that information. Two, I just gave you an example of being excited when you are telling something to someone who you are comfortable with. You can apply the same emotions and the speeds that go with them in situations other than just with people who you are within your comfort zone. What I like to see is the business presenter who gets excited in a meeting and his voice reflects that because he speeds up and slows down. That presenter is way more likely to get my business then the one who holds it together for the sake of professionalism. Just because you are in a business meeting does not mean you cannot get excited about something and speed up, no, keep it real. If that is what you would do in real life, then do it all the time. Here is an example, broken down of what I am talking about.

Example:

At/work/today/I/got/a/raise. (The dashes mean no space was really taken in between words, they were all rattled off very quickly).

Now could it be more interesting, more delicious if you incorporated both together.

(Spaces mean pauses or slow-downs)

At/work/today/I/got   a   r aaaaaise. Get the idea. Start playing with two things. Applying the same vocal qualities of speed that you would with your friends in all areas of your life and two mixing up fast and slow a little, always referencing the different shades of emotions making things not only more interesting, but not so predictable.

Now, before I leave fast and slow, I want to make a quick note about the people who speak extremely fast, you know who you are! You have to *slow down* so we can understand you. There is no point in you speaking at all if I can't understand what you're saying. With that said, there is just one problem. You, for the most part, can't tell when you're going fast or how fast you are going. I know this because I work with tons of people on speed and when I slow them down they think it's torture and when they speed up they think they are speaking at a reasonable pace.

So, several things have to happen. First, you have to breathe. Fast speakers are notorious NON breathers. Second, you have to think about and incorporate variety (the "big three") at all times. It is more important for you than any other student to work hard at incorporating the "big three." Why? Because if you are busy incorporating the "big three," then you will automatically slow down without thinking about it and for you, the fast speaker, the worst thing you can do is think about it.

Operative Words

"Operative words" is a fancy phrase that means putting more emphases on some words. When we have conversations with other people, people that are our friends or family, people that we are comfortable with, we do this automatically. When we are "on," we do not do it at all. We become on in many, many life situations because we are uncomfortable. The techniques that I am giving you will train you to automatically do all of these wonderful things...even when you are "on."

Okay, here is an example of operative words (they will be in capitals). This is how you might have a conversation, using operative words, automatically, while talking with one of your close friends or family.

Example:

"ARE you kidding me?" Is that what you would say after finding out that one of your friends is getting divorced and it came out of nowhere? Would you put for emphasis on "are" or would you say "Are you KIDDING me?" There is not always a right word to put the emphasis on. The point I'm trying to make in this moment is that something in each sentence you speak has to have more value; has to have a stress somewhere. Why? Because it makes it more interesting to listen to AND helps get your point across. Operative words help you get what you want.

When we talk about balance we have

to talk about value. When I use the word value I mean what a word is worth. In speech, there are two forms of value, individual words and separate sentences. First, within a sentence you cannot give every single word the same value. All the words cannot sound exactly the same if you want to be interesting. Something, anything, has to have more emphases.

Exercise Fifteen

Pay attention to how you use operative words as you speak in your daily life. What are the words you tend to put more stress on? Do you stress a lot of words, do you not stress any words at all, etc.

Writing Space for Exercise Fifteen

Try to imagine life without operative words, I mean in your conversations now, today. You wouldn't say, "The building is on fire," with no emphasis anywhere, now would you? No, you would say "The BUILDING is on FIRE" or possibly "THE BUILDING IS ON FIRE!!!" In that case stressing all the words is probably okay, and there are exceptions to rules. In general, some people swing to the opposite of not stressing enough words and they stress EVERYTHING. That's not good either. It is important to create a balance and the balance is created by stressing or emphasizing the most *important* words, the words with the most value, and the words that will ultimate communicate what YOU WANT.

At this point, now that we have a

sense of what your pattern is, too much, too little, etc, let's start playing around with emphasizing certain words in sentences more than others.

Exercise Sixteen

Practice sentences for emphasis. When you say these sentences, I want you to say each sentence over and over and each time emphasize a different word so you can begin to see how many options there are in stressing words. Ultimately, you want to stress the words that you think have the most value and will help you clearly express what you want to express.

Example:

Say this sentence over as shown.

How are YOU? (emphasis on "you")
HOW are you? (emphasis on "how")
How ARE you? (emphasis on "are")

Repeat that same pattern on all of the sentences listed below. It might be beneficial to write down how you finally decide to say the sentence, showing the stress you have chosen. If you are a visual learner this might help you see your pattern.

What do you want for lunch?

You want me to do what?

She told me that she was coming.

Don't even think about.

Where are your shoes?

The towels have been folded and are on the dryer.

If you buy this product I can guarantee you will make money.

I am asking you to be fair and honest with yourself.

Don't do it for me, do it for yourself.

Thank you for considering us as your service provider.

Tell me it isn't true.

Writing Space for Exercise Sixteen

In addition to operative words we also have to look at operative sentences. By this I mean, every single sentence cannot have the same value. Would you say these two sentences the same way, give them both the same value? What do you want for lunch? And The Building is on Fire. No you would not, so why is it that when you give a presentation or work with a client, patient or customer, or teach a class or develop a relationship, all of a sudden everything has the same value? Now I'm not saying the doctor needs to say, I'm sorry but YOU HAVE CANCER!!!! No, not at all, but some sentences do and should have more vocal value than others. In order to get what you want, which is sometimes simply just to be heard, some sentences have to make more of an impact than others.

Exercise Seventeen

Pay attention to what you do with your sentences. How much value do you give each sentence? Do you give each sentence the same value creating a monotone voice? Do you give too much emphasis to everything?

Writing Space for Exercise Seventeen

After completing exercise seventeen you should have a better sense of what you do with your sentences; where you assign too much value and where you do not assign enough value. The next exercise gives you some phrases so you can practice giving different value to different sentences in the same thought pattern. Practice these sentences the same way that you practiced the operative words. Try out different stresses on different sentences. You will know it when it sounds right because it feels right.

Exercise Eighteen

Practice sentences for variety in value.

I told her that I was not coming until later and she got really mad

about it. I can't just drop everything every time she wants me to.

In addition to 24 hour customer service, our sales reps are available to you by email and phone Monday through Friday from 9-8. After you buy our product, I can promise you that you won't be left on your own. We have the best customer follow up program of anyone in our market.

The writing assignment is long but beneficial. I don't want you to think of it as simply another assignment. I want you to put some thought into it. I want this assignment to be a spring board for your future.

I can't seem to understand what you're saying to me. Clearly, you and I communicate in such a different language that there is no way we can get on the same page. I'm willing to keep trying but you have to stop yelling at me.

The books are for sale and if you buy more than one you get a discount. Clearly, the more you buy, the deeper the discount. I recommend you buy an entire lot of 10. You might not need them now but trust me, these are the kinds of books you want to keep on the shelf for reference forever.

Writing Space for Exercise Eighteen

INFLECTION

Now in addition to operative words we have to take a look at inflection. The techniques are somewhat similar but yet different. Using operative words is putting emphasis on certain words where inflection is raising or lowering the pitch on certain words. As we work on inflection it becomes important to incorporate the section on operative words and emphasis along with pitch play.

There are certain words in which your pitch should automatically go up and certain words in which your pitch should automatically go down. If you do not put inflection on words you will sound monotone which is something I talk more about in the pitch section.

Now most of you probably put your

inflections on the proper words at the proper times but you might be surprised at how many people do not put any inflection anywhere or put inflection on the wrong words at the wrong times. What is actually more likely to happen is that people give an upward inflection to everything they say which then keeps their voice in a higher unnatural pitch range or makes some women sound like little girls, a big problem with pageant voices, actresses and often times business presenters.

Exercise Nineteen

Have someone listen to you for a day or a week and tell you what you inflection pattern is. If you would like and think you can do this activity on your own then get a tape recorder and tape yourself

speaking and see what your patterns of inflection are.

Writing Space for Exercise Nineteen

First of all I want to look at questions. Any and all questions generally end with an upward inflection or higher pitch.

Example:

Are you coming for dinner? Dinner would be raised a notch in pitch. What is she thinking? Thinking would be raised a notch in pitch.

Exercise Twenty

Try out these question sentences putting an inflection on the last word.

Where are you going?
Why is he doing that?
Can you get me the keys please?
Did she say she was coming?
Are you going to be able to go to

the party?
What are you wearing Friday?
What are we having for dinner?
Where did she go?
Did she have her baby?

Writing Space for Exercise Twenty

Now if you inflect every single sentence you say it is going to be imperative for you to practice questions and sentences saying them with a downward inflection on the last word.

Exercise Twenty One

Try out these sentences putting a downward inflection on the last word of the sentence.

I think I would like to go.
She may be coming over tomorrow.
They got a new puppy.
I met her in college.
For now, leave things as they are.
Do not forget to change the clocks tonight.

It's almost your birthday.
The water is very hot.
Dance lessons have been moved to Thursday evenings.

Writing space for Exercise Twenty One

Exercise Twenty Two

Using the sentences in the last two exercises, try out different inflection up and down, not necessarily directed in the activities themselves. Just play around with it to hear the different way things can sound.

Writing space for exercise twenty two.

Other sentences and statements that might require an upward inflection or higher pitch oftentimes are simple one word statements such as; well, don't, you say and so forth. The inflection, whether it is up or down is determined by the emotion behind the word.

Exercise Twenty Three

Say the following words first with upward inflection or downward inflection based on the emotion or feeling in parenthesis.

Well (I am waiting.)
my (I am surprised.)
oh (Is that so?)
oh (I am hurt that you said that to me.)
stop (Right there.)
go (On a red light.)

say (That is excellent.)
you (He meant you?)
you (He meant you.)
now (Do not wait.)

Writing Space for Exercise Twenty Three

Ultimately what you want to achieve with your inflection is a very fluid almost melodic way of speaking. Now, do not go too far and become singsong, in fact if you already have a singsong voice then you need to do all the above listed activities focusing on using more downward inflection to build up that part of your inflection repertoire.

Exercise Twenty Four

Try out the following sentences coming upward and downward inflection in each sentence. Start off each sentence in a regular speaking voice then follow the directions in parenthesis for the next part of the sentence to inflect either up or down.

I couldn't do it, (up) even for you.
He stopped still, (up) listening intently.
If they lose it, (down) they will never find it.
You can't lose, (up) take a shot.
If he doesn't answer, (down) call him.
Do you, (up) or don't you.
If you can't do it, (down) I can.

Writing Space for Exercise Twenty Four

Another element you want to incorporate with inflections is pausing controls.

Exercise Twenty Five

Try out these two word sentences. Between each of the two words, pause. Use a neutral voice on the first word always. First try out the two word combinations with the second word, after the pause, having a higher inflection. Then repeat all the two word combinations with the second word having a lower inflection. This is just to give you some practice and awareness of the possibilities of using high and low inflections.

move fast
shut up

**go home
wake up
stay here
fish swim
jack fell
right now
we heard
make way
look out
stay here**

Writing space for Exercise Twenty Five

TONE

When I talk about tone I am talking about the actual sound quality that your voice makes, or what the sound sounds like to others ears. Now, do not get this confused with high or low pitch; they are different. The tone is nasal, whining, etc. I am sure you have heard this statement before, "I don't like your tone of voice." Why would someone not like a nasally tone of voice? Well, what does nasality present as? Possibly whiny? Possibly irritating? What about a growling or harsh tone of voice? It presents as anger or irritation. Do not underestimate what can be read through the tone of voice.

The tone of voice that you want to project is one of kindness, approachability, friendliness, a tone that is nice to listen to. How do you project this tone of voice? Well, for one thing if you have a nasal quality you must do extensive work on downward pitch. The downward pitch exercises will pull your voice out of your nose, almost literally. The downward pitch exercises will also change your tone if you are a little bit whiny or have a little girl voice.

Another way you can work on tone is to clearly connect emotions to sounds. The exercise below will help you learn to connect clearly identifiable emotions and thoughts to sounds and words and will improve your tone.

Exercise Twenty Six

I want you to work with someone that you feel really comfortable with on this exercise. You are going to have a conversation with this person but you're basically the only one that is going to do any talking. I want you to tell this person stories, made up or true. But, the catch is that you can only talk in gibberish. Gibberish is a nonsense language that is comprised of not much more than sounds. Perhaps you might think it sounds like a foreign language because it is certainly not understandable. Now, if you happen to know another language, do not use it, that defeats the point of the activity. The object is to be able to express information, a story, and feelings to another person through tone. Tone will be the only way the person can figure out what your story is. Even though you have gestures and facial expressions to help you with your story, try to keep them at a minimum and work on getting the story told and understood through tone.

Writing Space for Exercise Twenty Six

PAUSING

When I talk about pausing there are many ways in which you pause and/or use pauses. Pausing helps establish your speaking rhythm. Do you speak without pausing, talking rapidly so all your thoughts and words flow together without giving the listener an opportunity to digest what you're saying? When you do pause does it reflect disorganization? Are you pauses used in such a way that you appear shy? Do your pauses reflect hesitation in answering questions? Do your pauses reflect meaningful thought process?

Pauses are important in order to allow your listener the time to process and digest what you're saying. However, there is such a thing as over pausing and of course there is under pausing as well. The pause is tremendously powerful. When you pause everything stops and everyone pays attention. Therefore, you do not want to just throw your pauses away all the time. The pause lets the listener know "Hey, I am getting ready to say something really valuable so you better pay close attention and listen up." What I mean by this is, do not just pause before any and everything you say. Save your pauses and use them for the most important things you say. Pauses have value just like I spoke about in the operative words section. You do not want to put them before everything you say, save them and use them when you want to set up something important.

Clearly if you are a fast talker, and even if you're not, there is truth to the concept that we speak faster when nervous. The pause becomes even more valuable if you find yourself nervous or because of nervousness speaking extremely fast.

Pauses can also be helpful so you can stop and think in a number of different situations. This brings me to a thought that I would like to interject at this moment. I want to share with you one of the most important things I have ever learned in my life and I think it will come in handy for you as you learn to improve your communication skills. There is tremendous power in the pen and tongue. What that means is that your words whether spoken or written in a letter, email, text, whatever, have tremendous power and you can never take them back once you put them out there. Be cautious in what you say or write; do not let emotions drive those words.

This is where the pause comes in. Use the pause to think before you speak or write; it can help you from making costly mistakes. Do not be afraid to use a pause, but just learn how and when to use the pause so that it is appropriate and intelligent in its presentation.

Exercise Twenty Seven

Practice applying pauses to the following sentence. Only pause where it is indicated in the sentence in parenthesis. This exercise will help you understand and feel what it feels like to pause only at important times.

Let's put the nuts into (pause) the basket.
A child with a cleft palate tends to omit (pause) consonants.

We cannot go outside it is (pause) raining
I believe that all humans are (pause) created equal.
There is no point in crying (pause) it will not change anything.
Bees really will not sting you (pause) unless they feel provoked.
Take the carrots (pause) and the cabbages from the basket.
Be careful (pause) not to frighten the butterflies.
My father (pause) takes me fishing every fall.
What seems fine at fifteen seems (foolish) at fifty.
The woman (pause) died in the fire.
There are so many homeless animals, it's really (pause) sad.
The heat this summer has truly been (pause) unbearable.
My tooth really (pause) hurts.
I really want (pause) this pageant.

I think she is (pause) so nice.
I cannot believe she (pause) did that.

Writing Space for Exercise Twenty Seven

Exercise Twenty Eight

Now, try out these sentences and you decide where to put the pauses.

My friends, I cannot thank you enough.
The puppy was without a mother.
The groundhog saw his shadow and went back into his hole.
Pizza is absolutely my favorite food if it has lots of cheese.
I don't think I will have time to get to the store.
I love the set up of your dorm room.
I think her family is coming into town for Thanksgiving.
In my opinion, the war on drugs needs a serious re hauling.
Music therapy is a wonderful related service for children with

autism.
Writing Space for Exercise
Twenty Eight

ELONGATION

Now we need to briefly discuss elongation and its role in deliciousness. Elongation is not what I consider one of the big three, but I do consider it to be interesting and add flavor to your speech pattern.

Once again, this is something that we do naturally in our daily conversations with our safe people. Elongation is simply holding out sounds for a longer period of time. Elongation is an element that really helps express emotion. We use elongation with emotions like surprise, fear, anger and others.

Examples:

You see a dog start to dart across the road in front of an oncoming car, you say, "NOOOOOOOOO." The "O" is elongated.

You are in a huge fight with your boyfriend and in anger you want him to leave your apartment, you say, "GEEEEEET out," or possibly, "GET OUT NOOOOOWWWW."

You are talking to your friend about the vacation that you are getting ready to take together, you say, "I am sooooo excited."

Unfortunately, we tend to not incorporate elongation into our speech patterns when we are "on." It is something that makes us more interesting and more natural, so I encourage you to be aware of how often you elongate words and the words you elongate when you are with your friends. Then pay attention to how much/when you elongate when you are "on." If you elongate when you're "on" and not in casual conversation or vice versa make note of it and figure out why. Why is it that you elongate your words and make them more interesting in one scenario or another and how can you do it in all of your communication? Figure out the hows and whys and start incorporating elongation into all your speech; it will make you more delicious.

Now, here is a note for you Southern girls. Southerners, I myself am one, have the ability to turn a one syllable word into a four syllable word without even thinking about it. Remember we are going for balance so if this is what you tend to do it will be important for you to reverse this activity. What I mean by this is, instead of awareness of and addition of elongation you will need awareness of and decrease of elongation.

EXERCISE Twenty Nine

Try out the following sentences. Try elongating different words in the sentences until you find the best word or two in each sentence to elongate, where it makes the most sense. I don't recommend elongating more than one or two words in each sentence. Remember we are going for balance and making things more interesting.

**Can you please help me with my science project?
I love the pizza at La Pizzaria.
I am going to Italy as a foreign exchange student next summer.
My sister is having a baby and it's**

a girl.
Denise has the cutest little dog I've ever seen and she carries him around everywhere in her purse, crazy.
Did you hear we are getting next Friday off for an unexpected teacher work day?
I really hope I win the lottery this Saturday, it's up to four million dollars, can you imagine.
Do you like to read?
Have you ever had dinner down by the river?
I wonder what kind of winter we are going to have this year, mild or really cold.
My friends are coming in from Florida to have Thanksgiving Dinner with us this year.
I absolutely want to see that movie because it sounds so unusual and not like the same old story line that every single movie seems to have.

My mother loves chocolate.

Writing space for Exercise Twenty Nine

ARTICULATION

This brings us to the last of the critical elements of a obtaining a delicious voice, articulation, commonly referred to as diction, but in laymen terms it means having your spoken words clearly understood. How many times in a day do you have to ask someone to repeat what they said because you can't understand them? I am not talking about accents, grammar, speed, or volume, nothing like that. I'm talking about plain and simple you can't clearly make out the words, the vowels and the consonants, that are forming the words and being sent out of the person's mouth. In order to have proper diction there are lots of things I could teach, but I want to just give you two important points/visuals.

First, words are made up of vowels and consonants; you have to think of both of them paying the same admission price so all the letters that make up the words should get an equal opportunity to get out of your mouth. This includes the ending consonants which create the biggest problem in bad articulation/diction. We get lazy and we get slangy, and before you know it don't becomes "don," walk becomes "wal," found becomes "fou," and on and on. That is why it is so hard to understand people. In the professional world especially, you have to have what you are saying, the words that are coming out of your mouth, understood. Once again, if I can't understand you, there is no point in you even speaking. So, it becomes critical for you to get the vowels and consonants out of your mouth. Now, it is because we are lazy and slangy that the words don't come out, but there is a physical reason as well.

First you need to know where the words form in your mouth. For some of you the words form in the back of your mouth, others the lips, others high in the mouth, others low. Everyone is different, but it's important to know where your words are forming, and where the sound is coming together before it comes out of your mouth. Once you know where this is then you can see just how far those sounds, those words, have to travel before they come out of your mouth. The idea here is that the words/sounds have to GET OUT of your mouth. If they stay in the back of your mouth or stuck on your lips or stuck to the roof of your mouth then guess what, I CAN NOT UNDERSTAND YOU. So I want you to visualize the words, the letters, the sounds, coming out of your mouth. Visualize the words physically traveling out of your mouth; into the universe for someone else to hear so they can buy our product, do what we want, marry us or whatever! *See* the words coming out of your mouth.

Now that you can visualize the words coming out it's time to learn to drop your jaw and open your mouth. Opening your mouth and dropping your jaw is the only way that the words are going to come out of your mouth and be understood. Like I have said before I work with tons of people on their voices and a very large percentage of them DO NOT open their mouths when they speak, much less drop their jaw.

Exercise Thirty

yawn
yawn
yawn

Writing Space for Exercise Thirty

By yawing you begin to stretch the muscles of your mouth and face and begin to become more comfortable with your mouth wide open. Many, many people are afraid to open their mouths wide because do not like for people to see their teeth, or worry about bad breath or for many other reasons. People start not opening their mouths when they speak, then it becomes a part of who they are. The next thing you know, you have spent years not opening your mouth, and not letting the words come out. If that happens, then guess what, the face and jaw muscles tighten up and then it not only hurts to fully open your mouth but those muscles have to be re-trained, just like all the other muscles we are re-training.

One of the best ways to learn to get the vowels and consonants out is to overemphasize, like I was talking about before. Let's push your over emphasizing words out of your mouth to the very right line because we want it to fall back in the middle. Right now, it's over on the far left for many of you.

Now, I am going to give you a word list that I want you to practice, on your own in the privacy of your own room. Practice these words by really opening your mouth as you speak them. This will train you to open your mouth and drop your jaw so that the words will begin to come out of your mouth and be understood.

This exercise, just like pretty much everything in this book, takes practice and repetition because, as I have said over and over, you are re-training muscles and training your body and mind to do something different, different from the way it has done it for 20, 30, 40 years or more. So be patient. I am often asked, "How do I apply this to regular conversation?" I say, "You don't." Don't make a conscious effort to apply, make a conscious effort to do, to retrain and then I promise you out of nowhere, one day, these things will just start happening. Sometimes in 10 days, sometimes in 30, it all depends on how much you work on it, how much you practice it but it WILL happen. I have never, in 20 years, worked with a student who just was not able to change their voice, not able to make these simple steps work, EVER.

Exercise Thirty One

Practice saying these words, allowing each and every letter to come out of your mouth, overemphasizing.

(Just a note, you might not want to practice this while speaking to anyone, you might feel uncomfortable. This is more of a "let me sit at home and practice my word list" kind of activity).

ounce
foundation
stunning
underwear
sound
believe
standing
stop
shout

make
sound
land
fantastic
strong
incredible
patience
doctor
slipping
puppy
understand
pounding
cleaning
participated
better
fancy
outrageous
placement
desk
parent
teacher
considering
flippant
discourage

butter
development

Writing Space for Exercise Thirty One

SLANG AND SLURR

Two big problems with the way people speak today, and not just young people, is that they use way to much slang and they slur or mumble their words. You, as a professional who wants respect, cannot do either.

Let's talk about slurring and mumbling first. These two things occur simply because you get lazy and you do not expend any energy to get the words out of your mouth. If you truly work on the articulation exercises in the previous section, where you spend a great deal of time over articulating, you should improve your lazy mouth. Articulation can mean two things. First, getting the words out of your mouth so they can be understood, and second, getting across the point you are trying to make.

I want you to visualize the words in your mouth. Words rest in a place in your mouth before they come out. Now, how far they come out of your mouth, well, that is up to you. I want you to visualize getting the words that are resting in your mouth, probably towards the back, up and out of your mouth. If you do not make much effort to get the words out and they are resting in the back of your mouth, without much effort they will barely make it to your lips and then just sort of drop out of your mouth and hit the floor. I need you to work a little harder than that. Regardless of where your words are resting in your mouth, which is actually placement and I do not go into that in this book, but regardless of where they are you have to get them up and OUT of your mouth; *see* the word extending past your lips. This will greatly help your articulation. Think of it this way. It is a movie and each letter that is in your mouth paid admission to that movie. Now, I live in New York City and movies are not cheap here. Each letter paid full price, each letter deserves to get out of your mouth, or see the movie if you will.

Now a word about slang, text talk, and poor grammar: Three different things, none of which you can ever use. This is one of those things that I recommend you change about yourself if you do any of the above. Just like the "on" voice that can fail you, these types of speaking can fail you as well by sneaking in when you least expect. Just go ahead and stop using these types of speech in all your forms of communication and get a good voice that you use all of the time. Slang is the same way; you must stop using slang in all of your communications so that it will not sneak in at an unexpected moment and cause you to lose the crown, the audition, the job, the contract and anything else you want.

First let's look at some definitions.

Slang: any words or phrases that you use in a certain culture or time period or community.

Example:

check ya later, y'all, you guys, that's sick and so forth...

Text talk: the way you speak to each other via text, primarily in abbreviations.

Example:

OMG, ttyl, :) LMAO and so forth...

Poor grammar (this one should be obvious): using words in an un-educated manner, or should I say proper context is a complete death sentence. If this is something you do, you should enroll in an English class or hire a speaking coach to work with you one on one ASAP. You will not EVER make it anywhere if you cannot articulate yourself as an intelligent lady. Proper grammar is crucial to be seen in this light.

Example:

I have tooken that test before.

EXERCISE Thirty Two

Have someone that is close to you, or perhaps not listen to you speak for a day, a week, however long it takes, (if they know you really well, they may not have to listen to you at all, they may already be able to answer this question) and then tell you if you use slang, poor grammar or text talk and if so what do you say/do. Write it down and become very aware of when you do it and not doing it anymore.

Writing Space for Exercise Thirty Two

Exercise Thirty Three

Spend about ten minutes every day saying the following tongue twisters over and over. Even if you don't slur or mumble they will be wonderful exercises to improve what the muscles in your face can do and will even improve already great articulation.

Red leather, yellow leather, red leather, yellow leather
She sells seashells by the seashore
unique New York unique New York
Betty bakes biscuits better than Barbara bakes bitter bread

Then I want you to pick about five consonants or more a day to practice with vowel sounds. The patter you will say out loud and clear is as follows with each consonant one at a time.

Fafa (long A/uh)
Fafa feefa (long E/uh)
Fafa feefa fifi (long I/uh)
Fafa feefa fifu fofa (long O/uh)
Fafa feefa fifu fofa foofa (long U/uh)

Then repeat with other consonants in the F position.
Great examples to use are B, R, K, S, T, D, and so on.

Baba
Baba, Beeba and so forth with as many consonants as you like, vowel sounds stay the same.

Writing Space for Exercise Thirty Three

IDIOSYNCRATIC SOUNDS AND WORDS

I will talk about idiosyncratic movements when I get to the movement section and I can assure you that you will have some of those, but for now we are going to address idiosyncratic sounds and words.

What do I mean by idiosyncratic words and sounds? Sounds or repetitions of words that you use, most likely, not even realizing you use them.

Idiosyncratic sounds are things like clicking your tongue, smacking your lips, sucking in air, heavy sighs and so forth. I mention heavy sighs because I am a heavy sigher and I did not even have any idea that I was. Once, during rehearsal for a touring show I was doing, an actor said to me, "Do you know you sigh all the time?" I, of course, denied it saying, "No I don't." Well, guess what, I started paying attention to myself and boy oh boy was I in for a surprise, I sigh all of the time, or I did until it was brought to my attention and then I worked on stopping. The point is, you very well could have an audible sound that you do and not even know you do it. Ask around, your friends, family, anyone you spend a decent amount of time with and ask them if they have heard you making any of these idiosyncratic sounds. You may find out that no one can tell you if you do this or not, so you may need to ask them to listen to you for a while to see.

The important thing is that you find out if you have one and what it is, just like me and my sighing. Awareness is absolutely the first step in changing anything about you, especially a habit and that is exactly what idiosyncratic behavior is, whether it is sounds or words or gestures or ticks.

It is also highly possible that you use idiosyncratic words. Almost everyone, but especially young people, use idiosyncratic words when they speak. What I am talking about here is using words or even sayings repetitively and possibly not even in context.

Examples of idiosyncratic words and phrases:
Okay
Like (this one is very popular)
For sure
I know-right

Exercise Thirty Four

Repeat the same process as you did for the sounds, ask people closest to you to pay attention to see if you have any words that you use repetitively or out of context. If the people you ask to help you do not automatically notice certain words or repetitions then ask them to listen to you for a while to help you discover any of these words. Write them down. Become very aware of when you use them and start working on NOT using them.

Writing Space for Exercise Thirty Four

As I said before, it is highly possible you are not aware that you even use idiosyncratic sounds words, but I recommend you find out because they are another death sentence for you if you want to have a great voice whether it be in casual conversation or the audition or the interview process and so forth. Idiosyncratic words and phrases cannot be used at all because it does not make you sound intelligent, classy, or the way an excellent representative for an entire country or group of people should sound.

Again, like so many other things including being "on," you have to remove these sounds and words completely from your speaking skills because you do not want them to crop up and sneak in, which could happen, especially if you are nervous. It is just one more element that should become a part of how you communicate, not something that you have to think about.

DIALECTS

I want to just briefly talk about dialects. Now, some would disagree with this but, I believe if you have a strong dialect whether it is Southern or Bronx New York or whatever region it is, it is in your best interest to either reduce it or get rid of it completely. I am not saying you have to, but if it is strong enough to be a distraction or affects your overall speaking and presentation skills, it needs to go. Again, as a professional, you are going to come into contact with and often times represent a large group of people, not just the South or the North etc... You must represent the all, the whole, like the "all American girl" or the "girl for all the people" or all "teen girls." Dialects can also be subtle suggestions of class, age, sophistication, education level and so forth. This means that dialects can also cause prejudice and unconscious associations that might not be positive. We live in a global world now more than ever. In everything you do you will encounter a variety of different accents. It is in your best interest for numerous reasons to be as neutral as possible.

Here is an example of negative reflection stemming for dialects. Many of my clients are from the South and they want to reduce or completely get rid of their Southern accent. Why? It has been there experience that in business many people in the country or the world have an impression of Southerners because of their dialect. They are considered and treated as not intelligent, sometimes even ignorant. The same can hold true for a Northern accent but with different impressions. My northern clients want to reduce their accents so they will not sound so harsh or edgy.

With that said, in my opinion, the ONLY way to reduce accents is by learning proper placement. If you try and reduce your accent by listening to tapes of neutral dialects and listen to and basically memorize the sounds from the tape, you will NOT be able to achieve consistency when you try to speak with a new accent. It is essential, just like everything else I have talked about so far, that you train your muscle memory in knowing how to properly place the sounds. I am not going to go into great detail about accent reduction. If you would like further instruction on this and proper placement, feel free to contact me and I can point you in the right direction.

Exercise Thirty Five

Now, I do not recommend this type of exercise often, however, for you and what you are doing here I am going to recommend it. I want you to spend some time taping yourself speaking. I don't want you to get to critical or make this too crucial of an exercise but I want you to tape yourself, maybe in a casual situation and if possible a speaking situation. After you have taped yourself, listen and see what you think. Like I said, do not be over critical and go crazy trying to change things that you are not even sure are right or wrong/good or bad just see if anything stands out. If it does, make a note of it and find the place in this book where it talks about whatever it is that you found that you did not like and GET RID OF IT!

Writing Space for Exercise Thirty Five

MOVEMENT

The goal with movement which is gestures, posture, facial expression and what you do with your eyes, just like the voice, is to make it delicious. When I talk about delicious movement, I am talking about *fluid* movements, gestures, calm, relaxed facial expressions, and correct use of eyes. You have probably seen the person that flows into the room like liquid. It is difficult to take your eyes off of them and every move they make is almost like watching a ballet.

Non-verbal communication or what I call movement reinforces your position, attitudes, and implicit beliefs and unconsciously suggests whether you are submissive or dominant, spontaneous or controlled and trusting or wary. Movement speaks volumes, so it is very important for you to be aware of what you do and ultimately work towards making the right movement choices in both casual conversation and public speaking.

Now when we talk about "movement" or delicious movement to be more exact we must take a look at several different things. As I said before, the areas we have to address are posture, gestures, facial expressions, and the eyes. I will break them down one by one.

Posture: Your posture must represent someone who is confident but not cocky, friendly with tremendous class.

There are many choices in posture, things that you might possibly do or could do. Here are some stance/posture examples of what you DO NOT want to do: stiff, slumped, angled torso, shoulders forward, angled head, pelvis tilt, twisted, slouching, cringing, tightness, towering and forward jaw.

Gestures: Your gestures must be used appropriately to accent the words you use to communicate and to express feelings such as sincerity, friendliness, compassion, diplomacy, warmth and confidence. Be careful of gestures which express anger, hostility; know it all attitude, dishonesty, not trustworthy and so on.

Face: Your facial expressions are strong indicators of mood, stress level, nervousness and how you are feeling about situations and people. It is important to learn to have a stress free, relaxed face that utilizes expressions which are inviting, kind, compassionate, intelligent, good judgment, charming, sincere, friendly, witty, tact and confidence.

In addition, you also must be aware of something with your face called indicating. I will talk about that more extensively in the face section.

Eyes: Your eyes should reveal the true feelings of the heart and really are the windows to the soul. What you do with your eyes can reflect not only the kind of person that you are you which is hopefully kind, compassionate and honest but also your true feelings about people and situations.

All movement or non-verbal behavior gives messages. It is imperative that you learn to give the correct messages with your body and your face and eyes.

Exercise Thirty Six

It is essential that you practice doing movements, gestures, sitting and facial expressions and eyes expressing the above listed types of movements. I want you to actually over exaggerate these movements, not for the same reason I have you over-do your voice, these I want you to overdo so you can get a very good feel for what these movements feel like so you can determine if they are familiar to you or not, so you can make sure and feel what it feels like to feel these emotions in motion.

Writing Space for Exercise Thirty Six

POSTURE

First things first, we begin with posture. Now, I have talked about posture before in reference to stacking building blocks and the importance and value of that. Just as when you are learning new vocal techniques and it feels strange, the same thing will occur with correct posture and learning to stack the building blocks or posture blocks if you will one on top of the other. Just make sure your shoulders are not too far back or too far forward, that is the key.

Another thing to pay attention to with your posture is that you are not sucking your stomach in, which if you're breathing properly and stacked correctly, this will not be an issue.

Make sure you place your head properly on top of your shoulders when stacking your blocks; you do not want it to far back or too far forward and you must have your shoulders and knees relaxed. As strange as it may sound, those are two places where you tend to tense up when nervous and those are two places that can be noticeable if you tense them up. The knees can lock up and once you lock tour knees nothing can flow, your breath, your voice, your emotions or personality. In addition, you can pass out if your knees are locked and you certainly cannot walk gracefully if they are.

But, perhaps even worse is shoulder tension. If you tense up your shoulders, they actually raise up. I want you to spend a week watching your shoulders. Shoulder tension in posture and the raising of the shoulders may turn out to be one of those idiosyncratic things you do not even realize that you do and when you spend some time looking at it you will see, in horror, just what kind of contorts you do with your body.

Exercise Thirty Seven

Watch your posture and your body and see where you are holding in the tension and if the tension is altering any body parts to make them look abnormal or are distorting the perfectly stacked up building blocks.

Writing Space for Exercise Thirty Seven

GESTURES

Movements also express emotions based on whether or not they are jerky, pressured, gradual, easy, tense, fatigued, graceful, shaky, deliberate, furtive, clumsy and more.

We will now start with my favorite and specialty movement, gestures. I love working with people on their gestures. First, I want to talk about idiosyncratic gestures. Similar to sounds or words you may say, often you are not even aware of them. However, there is probably a pretty good chance that you random gestures or movements are something you use. Now, when I talk about idiosyncratic gestures I am generally talking about movements or gestures you do without realization of them.

Before you begin thinking about idiosyncratic gestures, I want to clear something up. Having idiosyncratic gestures is different than being a hand talker or motionless, I will address those types of movements more later on but to give you an idea of what you could be looking at, the person who is the hand talker you have to tone down your gestures, and for the person that does no gesturing we have to give you some gestures which will make you more interesting and believe it or not, more natural. What I mean by hand talker is the person who uses their hands heavily when they talk; constant flailing of the hands is always going on. The person who does not use gestures is the person that can absolutely talk forever and never move their hands, at all, some of these people do not even make facial expressions.

But first let us look at idiosyncratic gestures.
Examples:

brushing your hair behind your ears, flapping your hands, clicking your fingernails, pulling your ear, tapping your fingers, rolling a pen or another object between your fingers, etc...

Exercise Thirty Eight

Just like with your voice, if you do not know if you use any gestures constantly then ask someone to tell you, if they don't know then ask them to pay close attention to you when you talk to them for a week or so. Write down what they observe or even gestures or movements that you are already aware you do.

Writing Space for Exercise Thirty Eight

Now, gestures are important, why? Because all gestures send a message, they all have meaning. Remember this; every single gesture means something and every single gesture you use says something about you as a person. Gestures are VERY IMPORTANT, clues to the kind of person that you really are so it is very important to know what gestures you use, what they say about you and which gestures you should use in order to present yourself in the best light.

First, I want to get rid of any idiosyncratic gestures.

Before we start adding in new gestures, I want you to get rid of any gestures you do repetitively, especially if they are annoying, which includes most idiosyncratic gestures. In order to get rid of these gestures one of the first things I have my students do is sit on their hands. Yes, you read that right. I want you to sit on your hands whenever you are talking to anyone. The reason for this is I want to start with a clean slate so I have to get you to stop doing everything that you currently do. This is also an activity that becomes essential for hand talkers. Repetitive movements/gestures are often times created from nervousness and then they become habitual and then you are no longer aware of them. It is that lack of awareness, the fact that these gestures have become such a part of you that breaking them can be quite difficult.

After completion of exercise thirty eight, you are now very aware of these gestures and desperately want to use them but they most totally be stripped away. Sit on your hands until you can carry on a conversation without using any gestures, especially the not so good ones! When you are sitting, sit on your hands. If you're standing clasp your hands together in front or behind your body. It may take weeks to get you to stop these idiosyncratic gestures but you have to get rid of them in order to start building a delicious gesture base.

Now, let us take a look at those of you who are hand talkers. Now, this is a very important part of how you express yourself and I do not want to have to remove this part of you, but, it is essential. Why? Because hand talking is very distracting and it gives the message that you are nervous. Being nervous is a message that you do not want to give, ever. The best and only way to get you to stop talking with your hands is very similar to stopping the repetition of negative gestures. You have to sit on your hands every time you're sitting down talking or if you're standing, clasp your hands in front or behind you. Another tactic that you can use, which can also be useful for getting rid of idiosyncratic gestures, is to keep a tally of how often you use your hands. Get a timer and have a conversation first, with someone you are very comfortable with, then have a conversation with someone you are not that comfortable with. If a timer is too obvious or not an option then try to use your watch to get a rough idea, it does not have to be exact. Plan to talk for about fifteen to thirty minutes give or take. When you are talking to both people, the one you know well, the one you are very comfortable around, and the one you are not so comfortable around, keep a mental tally of how many times you fling your hands around. I think you will find that you are constantly flailing your hands whether you know it or not. Many hand talkers are very aware that they use their hands repetitively but some are not. Awareness will be the first step towards stopping the story telling you do with your hands. You might find that you flap more when you're comfortable; you might find the opposite to true. It does not matter either way; the hand talking has to stop. However, if you hand talk more with the person you are not as comfortable with it is very telling that you do this when you are nervous. If that is the case, then you need to be hyper vigilant about this because pageant interviews are situations in which you will tend to be more nervous. Of course, I am hoping that after you have mastered all of the elements in this book you will never be nervous again. Why? Because you will feel so comfortable with your voice and I know your self-esteem is going to dramatically improve after you see so many changes in your voice and body.

Now if you do not gesture at all it is essential that you add gestures when you are conversing. Believe it or not there are many people who never ever use their hands when they are talking. In a way you are one step ahead of the process because you do not have to get rid of anything, however, when we build your gesture base you may find it even more difficult to gesture because it does not feel comfortable to you. So as far as taking gestures away, do not worry, you have nothing to take away and I am not going to make you flap your hands about just to get them moving.

So, now we have gotten rid of all the idiosyncratic gestures and the hand talkers have learned how to keep their hands still. What do we do now? Now we build a delicious gesture base. Remember before when I was talking about the country club buffet and the dollar menu? This application could not be more perfect for the use of gestures. What kinds of gestures do you want, dollar menu or country club buffet? I certainly hope you said country club buffet because those are the most delicious. Now, the most important thing to know here is that I AM NOT trying to make you use gestures that you do not feel comfortable with, not at all, that will make things much worse.

Now there are lots and lots of gestures and they all mean something. Below is a list of some of the common gestures and what they mean. When I say what they mean, I mean, the message they give to the person you are communicating to your audience. Ideally what we want to do here is get rid of all gestures with negative connotations and replace them with interesting, delicious ones. But first let's take a look at the not so delicious gestures or what I refer to as the dollar menu gestures.

Smiling

Smiling: Represents friendliness, but continuous smiling without stopping makes people think your hiding something. In addition, there are several types of smiles, natural or forced and fake. I encourage you to work on your natural smile as it will represent friendliness. A fake smile will be obvious due to the tension in your face and will portray you as not real, not approachable, and not sincere. The best smiling is intermittent smiling because that draws the listeners into what you are saying. In addition, intermittent smiling shows that you are more natural, approachable and most likely telling the truth.

Hands:

Rubbing your palms together: tells others that you are expecting something good to occur, this is generally a positive gesture.

Clenched hands: if they are loosely clenched, it indicates confidence and a relaxed state of mind which is a good thing but tightly clenched hands reveal that a person is frustrated or has a hostile attitude. In addition, loosely clenched hands in front of the face or on the table reveal a positive state of mind but tightly clenched hands below the stomach area can make others believe that you are thinking negatively.

Palms together with fingertips of each hand touching each other lightly, almost like you are forming a triangle with your hands, means to others that you have a know-it-all attitude, definitely not something you want to portray.

Palms facing upwards as you freely use your hands can also indicate a know- it-all attitude and also can show greed, like you want or expect things from others.

Palms facing downward as you move your hands about however, indicates you are willing to listen and take orders which is an excellent gesture.

Palms gripped or hands held together behind your back can signify superiority and confidence. Now confidence is a great thing to portray but superiority, not so much, so be careful about how much you use this gesture. This also represents fearlessness, this is good for stressful situations because it can make you feel more at ease and boost confidence.

Palm in palm gesture almost as if you were in a clapping position but not clapping and hands on hips both indicate superiority and confidence as well. I encourage people to keep their use of hands on hips to a minimum. I do not think it reads all that bad but it's just not as interesting as other gestures you can make.

Folded Arms:

Firm arms folded across the chest means that you feel threatened, nervous, negative, and have a defensive attitude. Even if you are cold, stay away from this one, no matter what. This is also a very habitual gesture that many people use so if you are one of those people you must break this habit.

Folded arms across your chest with your thumbs out indicates that you believe you are superior to others.

Folded arms across your chest with your fists firmly clenched indicate hostility. This is a gesture that you often see people do in conflict.

Partial arm cross, perhaps where your arms are not folded up across your chest but are laying on each other, shows lack of confidence. I would avoid this one as well.

Crossed arms with your arms folded into each other shows that you are completely closed off and possibly defensive. Definitely you do not want people to perceive you as closed off. It is important for people to see you as approachable and body language is almost solely responsible for creating this image.

Open arms or arms just hanging by your sides shows that you are inviting and non-threatening. Your arms hanging by your side is a great choice, but for some of you, this will be a hard gesture to do until you get used to it.

Legs:

Crossed legs at the knees show you to be defensive, similar to crossed arms. It is often times better to cross legs at the ankles or to simply just put your feet on the floor side by side.

Shoulders:

Hunched over shoulders represent that you are introverted and drawn into yourself; it says to people that you do not want to be bothered.

Head:

Bowed head completely shuts people out.
Sharp head tilts show that you are bored.

Slight tilting of the head represents that you are interested in the other person and interested in hearing what they have to say, this is a good choice just do not overuse it.

Face and Eyes:

Blank expression on your face shows a sign of hostility or possibly that you are not listening because you are thinking of what you want to say next.

Frequent eye contact shows others that you are telling the truth. This is very important to do. If for any reason you do not make constant eye contact you must learn to do so, immediately.

Looking away and not making eye contact tells others that you are dishonest, not telling the truth and are a shady character. By looking away you can also show the other person you are talking to that you do not believe what they are saying.

Looking to the left if you make a statement or if the person you are talking to looks to the left on speaking shows that you are not telling the truth.

Scratching your chin shows that you do not believe the person you are talking with. In addition, playing with one of your ears expresses the same feeling.

Now here are a few more gestures that you want to make sure you do not make a part of your delicious gesture repertoire.

Shaking or pointing a finger shows that you think you're superior and that you are angry and scolding. Biting fingernails represents nervousness, insecurity and low self-esteem.

Wringing of hands shows you are anxious or anticipating something as well as nervousness.

Tugging, smoothing or playing with hair represents lack of self-confidence and insecurity.

Rubbing your nose represents that you are rejecting the person you are talking to or what is being said, there is doubt or that you are lying.

Squirming in your seat or fidgeting with your hands expresses nervousness, boredom and possibly dishonesty.

Narrowing eyes expresses that you

are suspicious.

Placing your hand to your cheek shows that you are evaluating or thinking.

This is a nice gesture to use occasionally, at the appropriate time.

Raising eyebrows shows you are cautious or suspicious.

Clenching fist expresses anger and hostility.

Rubbing your eyes shows you are in disbelief or doubt the person you are talking to or what is being said.

For the most part I have just given you a long list of gestures that, well, you should not use. So you say, "Well, gosh, all of those gestures have negative connotations so what kind of gestures can I do, what are the gestures that will show me in a positive light?"

First of all, country club buffet gestures, positive representations of you, are unique and different. Country Club buffet gestures make a statement and they should reflect your true feelings and your personality. Remember more than anything, in order to wear the crown you have to have a great personality. Gestures can help you express just how great your personality is.

Example:

Imagine you are pondering something, perhaps the person you are speaking with has said something to you and you want to reflect on what has been said. A delicious gesture might be a slight head tilt with a nod or possibly clasping the hands at chest level, or even better, what about moving your hand in a little swirl on the table as if you were drawing a circle? That gesture is more interesting and different, not something that you see every day, something that sets you apart from everyone that is doing the obvious randomness that most people do with their bodies.

Before I continue on to examples of delicious gestures, I want to make a note about the movement origin of truly effective gestures. Effective gestures actually start from the shoulder, not the elbow or the wrist. All delicious gestures should stem from your shoulders in order to be a fluid movement that is an extension of your body. Gestures whose point of origin is the shoulder are not only more fluid but they are more powerful. But, perhaps the best thing about starting your gestures from your shoulders will help release upper body tension, remember those shoulders I talked about?

Now, for your consideration, here are some examples of delicious gestures or country club buffet gestures. Remember you can create your delicious gestures by following the guidelines laid out in this section.

Hands in front of mid-section, loose fingers, palms toward your body: Reinforcement of what you are saying verbally
Example: you're talking about tall and so you use your hands to show tall. As long as you do not overdo it, these types of gestures can be okay.

Palms up with hands at the mid-section are a wonderful choice.

Hands at mid-section, palms facing in, fingers touching, almost like praying hands but not vertical, horizontal.

Hands loosely clasped up at chest level.

Circles of any kinds with fingers, hands, etc... is always beautiful and soothing.

Hands at mid-section, palms down, vertical movements side to side.

Hands down by sides.

Hands at mid-section, palms up.

A slight placement of the hand on your face.

Slightly brushing your hair away.

Lightly touching breastbone with hand/fingertips.

Clasped hands under the chin with chin resting lightly on them.

Now you just have to start exploring with things that feel right and look interesting, things that express who you are and how you feel; movements and gestures that make an impression and an impact. When you are watching yourself create your gestures ask yourself "Does this gesture look threatening or does it look friendly, approachable, inviting. What does this gesture say about me? What emotion does this gesture express?"

Exercise Thirty Nine

Come up with as many unusual but not weird gestures that you can think of. Stay away from the obvious gestures that you see all of the time such as crossing arms, tapping foot, wringing hands and so on...This will be your new gesture base. The gestures that you come up with you will want to start using as often as you can. The more you practice with them, the more you will feel comfortable with them and discover if they work for you or not.

Writing Space for Exercise Thirty Nine

It should be clear from the gestures I listed and what they represent that gestures clearly are physical representations of feelings and emotions. Therefore, it is important to create gestures that fit the emotions you want to express. Sometimes it is not always clear how you feel simply by what you are saying and how you are saying it. Gestures are for that very purpose, to help others understand what you are saying and how you feel about it. Just always remember, body language is more powerful and telling than the words you speak and how you speak them. Some might even say, "Actions speak louder than words."

Exercise Forty

Come up with an interesting gesture to express how you feel about the following list of events or emotions. Once again, do not come up with the obvious, the gestures that you see everyone else doing.

You are running late.
You are hungry.
You are angry.
You are sad.
You are giving orders or directions to someone.
You are tired.
You are hot.
You are deep in thought.
You are pondering.

PART II of this Exercise is to identify emotions or rather how you feel when you execute the following gestures written below. How does it make you feel to do the following?

**Shake your fist.
Point your finger.
Rub your forehead.
Wring your hands.
Cross your arms.
Snap your fingers one time.
Clasp hands behind your back.
Tap your foot.
Drum your fingers on a table.**

**Writing Space for Exercise 40
Parts I and II**

Exercise Forty One

Once again you are going to work with someone you are comfortable with. Practice telling stories whether they are made up or true to someone only using gestures, no words. The object here is to see how clearly you can communicate/express yourself with just your gestures, facial expressions and eyes.

Writing Space for Exercise Forty One

Bad gestures and movements can be un-learned, in fact they MUST be un-learned and new ones put in their place. Here are some examples of great activities that will help you create awareness of your poor gestures so that you can ultimately get rid of them and replace them with good choices.

Exercise Forty Two

Role Reversal
Play a scene, which is basically nothing more than everyday conversation with someone whom you feel comfortable with. But, have them play you. You can play them or anyone else but you cannot play yourself. The person who is playing you must act exactly as you do, so you are going

to have to do this activity with someone who knows you pretty well. The object of the game is for you to see yourself in action and feel how your movements impact others.

Writing Space for Exercise Forty Two

Exercise Forty Three

Exaggeration

Again you will play a scene with someone who knows you very well. This time you will get to be yourself. But, what happens during this conversation is the person you are playing the scene with points out gestures and non-verbal behaviors that you do that are less than appealing. When these behaviors are pointed out, you must then overuse them and exaggerate them as much as you can. The object of the game here is to make you fully aware of the behaviors and gestures that you want to get rid of by overemphasizing them in order to magnify them. By magnifying them you will then be aware of them when you even slightly execute them.

Writing space for Exercise Forty Three

Exercise Forty Four

Attitude Scene Play

You may do this exercise with someone who knows you very well or do it alone in front of a mirror. You will play yourself during this exercise. Before you do this exercise you will need to write down attitudes on separate sheets of paper.

Example attitudes:

kind
rude
snooty
sophisticated
better than
and so forth.

One at a time you will select a slip

of paper with an attitude written on it. Start to have a conversation acting out the "attitude" that is on your sheet. (If you are uncomfortable talking to yourself in front of a mirror, then do this activity with another person). Pay close attention to what you do with your body, gestures when portraying this attitude. Do you like what you see? Try to play the attitude again using different gestures, create gestures that are not so harsh or strong or flamboyant or weak or whatever your gestures were the first time you played the attitude.

Just remember, when working on creating gestures, you never ever want to create gestures that are super obvious to the audience. It is insulting and that is part of the problem with the gesture base that most people work with; it is too obvious and therefore it is insulting to the viewer. Do something interesting with your gestures rather than the same obvious thing that everyone else is doing.

Example:

Looking at your watch when you want to know what time it is or tapping your foot when you're waiting on the train.

What else can you do to represent those "attitudes" which might be irritation or nervousness, other than the obvious, which is possibly what you did the first time around?

Writing space for Exercise Forty Four

FACE

Now let's talk about your face for moment. One of the biggest problems I see in faces is tension. When you are tense you do one of the deadly sins of preventing deliciousness and that is indicating. When I talk about indicating it is something that can also happen when you are "on." What is indicating? It is when your facial muscles are tight and forced so you make extra effort to express your feelings, whether you realize you are doing it or not.

Most importantly, however, your facial expressions can, should, and usually do express your true feelings, often times whether you want them to or not. For example, when you really wanted to win and someone wins, you have to express happiness in your face, which is probably quite the opposite of how you truly feel. In this situation you would indicate or force happiness. If you truly want to be delicious you have to let that tension go from your face and call upon joy and let it shine through. If you do not have a tense, rock hard muscle face you will be able to make a more natural expression regardless of the emotion behind it.

Emotions are read on your face, whether you realize it or not and there are so many emotions that your face can tell about; sad, anxious, sleepy, amused, pouting, confused, pensive, warning, startled, barely tolerant and of course joy and happiness...that is where the smile comes in and of course as we learned earlier your smile must be genuine and not a plastered on fake smile that never goes away. This is somewhat an example of indicating. You constantly smile without cause and so the muscles of your face are tight to hold the smile. It is as if your face is hitting me over the head with a hammer saying, "I am friendly and happy, dang it!" That is what indicating is. So relaxation is important for many, many things but it is essential for your facial muscles to be relaxed. Indicating is insulting to the person who you are communicating with and says nothing but fake, fake, fake.

Exercise Forty Five

Practice the following facial exercises every single day and make them a part of your warm up routine before and during presentations and auditions and any other time you feel anxiety. Do all of the face exercise/warm

ups gently, do not over emphasize or over work any of your face muscles.

Scrunch up your face, relax, scrunch, relax
Pucker lips and relax, pucker and relax
Raise and lower eyebrows
Drop your jaw by opening your mouth really wide then close, then open, then close and so forth
Gently massage the muscles of your face

Writing Space for Exercise Forty Five

Exercise Forty Six

In front of a mirror, practice using combinations of muscles around the forehead, eyes, mouth, tilting the head, eye gaze and jaw. While looking in the mirror, create the facial expressions that you want to use to create the attitude you want to express. Create your facial expression buffet right in front of the bathroom mirror. Create ones that work and feel comfortable and give a sense of who you are. Don't make selections that are faked or have any negative or pretentious connotations to them.

Possible options to practice:
smiling
thinking
happy
confidence
knowledgeable

class
energized

And any others you would like to work on.

Writing Space for Exercise Forty Six

CASUAL CONVERSATION

When we talk about public speaking we are referring to two totally different things. There is public speaking which is more formal, like your pageant interview, and there is casual conversation which is more of when you are just talking to people. It is essential to master both. Why? Because you are going to encounter people all the time, you never know who they are or what they have to offer you. You always want to make a good impression and if you have a great voice and movements to match, if you always command the most attention in the room then everyone is going to want to be near you. Once that happens, the networking opportunities will be almost more than you can handle.

There are numerous ways you can

improve your ability to shine in casual conversation. First, casual conversation must be just that, casual conversation. So it becomes essential for you to be completely comfortable talking to anyone about anything, regardless of what kind of reciprocation you receive from the person you're conversing with. In order to do this, several things must occur. First, you must talk to people, many people, all the time. Next, it is important that you learn to not let emotions affect the way you respond to people. This can be important in public speaking Q & A and interviewing as well. What I mean by this is that regardless of what people say to you, you cannot lose your cool, snap, get angry, disrespectful etc. Now I am NOT saying be a doormat and I am certainly not saying you have to agree with what everyone says to you or change your viewpoints to make them happy (more on this later) but I am saying that you cannot let people rattle you. One of the sure fire ways for people to know that they have rattled you is through your body language, especially your face and eyes and your tone of voice. Regardless of whether you want to slap someone or not, you cannot let them know that. So, the work that you do on facial muscle relaxation and tone of voice is mandatory. That is just one of the many reasons that you need to speak to everyone you can, all the time, all walks of life. If you spend a great deal of time talking to people, surely, eventually, someone will be a jerk or make you mad. Take this experience as a wonderful opportunity to keep your cool and to keep your face and your voice from showing any type of disapproval. Take these opportunities as great times to express how you feel about certain subjects and topics and still keep your cool. That is called tact and diplomacy.

Remember these two things, forever, memorize them, practice them, and believe them. Tact and diplomacy are going to be valuable tools for you in all types of conversation, casual, formal, public speaking speeches, and interviews, everything you do. Tact and diplomacy will also help you for the rest of your life, in all areas.

Tact and diplomacy are like class, something that unfortunately does not exist like it used to but if you have it, you will stand apart from everyone else and that is a good thing. Class means you are able to carry yourself as a confident, friendly, polite person that has a backbone and an opinion, but expresses them with dignity, without foul language or raised volume or obscene and offensive hand gestures and body language.

Exercise Forty Seven

Every single day strike up a conversation with someone you don't know. Actually, do this as many times as you can. Talk to the checkout girl at the grocery store, the librarian, the convenience store worker, anyone, and everywhere you go. You must get comfortable talking to strangers. Remember, the casting director or whomever you're in front of most likely will be strangers as well, the more practice you have talking to

strangers the more it will become natural and when you meet the person you are trying to impress, it will be obvious that you are at ease with strangers.

In addition, when you are talking to strangers, feel free to practice any of the other skills that you are working on at the time. Remember, you might not ever see them again. Also, focus on eye contact, listening, turns taking and really caring about the conversation that you are having with this stranger.

Writing Space for Exercise Forty Seven

HUMOR

A word about humor: What can I say about humor? First and foremost, if you're not funny, don't try to be. Second, humor is a wonderful thing and can really be used to your advantage in high tension or flubbed up situations.

Some rules about humor: Always make sure the humor that you use is tactful, not bawdy, harsh, or offensive. Just because you think something is funny does not mean it is appropriate. Remember that, it may be funny but is it appropriate for all audiences? Also, just remember, you may think your funny, but make sure everyone else does as well.

Humor is not something that you force. If you are good at using humor you know that you simply release the humorous line, statement, or facial expression but you don't think about it. If you spend time thinking about how to get the humor in, then it probably won't work. Humor should only be used naturally. Some people are very good at using humor and some people are not. If you are not one of the people that has success with humor, possibly stay away from using it. The worst kind of use of humor is the person who thinks they are funny but they really are not. I do not see this too much in pageant girls but it can happen. No matter how hard it might be to know the truth, ask someone close to you to honestly tell you if you're funny or if you're one of those people who thinks they are funny and really are not.

One of the most important things

about humor is learning to laugh at you. That is a very important tool because it makes you human, just like everyone else. Also, laughter, laughing at yourself, is a wonderful way to release tension for you and others.

AFTERWARDS

There you have it. You are now armed with all the techniques, all the steps it takes to Be Delicious! I believe that if you executed every exercise in this book and if you mastered all of the elements you will truly succeed. I know that your chances of nailing the audition or the interview or getting the bid are much greater now than they were before you studied this book. But, I want you to know that you have begun to prepare yourself to succeed in all areas of your life. Great communicators are successful at everything they do and everyone wants to have what they have. Good job!

I wish you the best of luck and if you ever have any questions or concerns please feel free to contact me at msgcreativedrama@gmail.com and you can also see what's new at www.msgcreativedrama.com